W9-AMR-991

Student Handbook to Sociology

Deviance and Crime

Volume VI

Student Handbook to Sociology

Deviance and Crime

Volume VI

GLENN W. MUSCHERT

Liz Grauerholz
General Editor

☑ Facts On File
An Infobase Learning Company

Student Handbook to Sociology: Deviance and Crime
Copyright © 2012 Glenn W. Muschert

Facts On File, Inc.
An Imprint of Infobase Learning
132 West 31st Street
New York NY 10001

Library of Congress Cataloging-in-Publication Data

Student handbook to sociology / Liz Grauerholz, general editor.
    v. cm.
  Includes bibliographical references and index.
  Contents: v. 1. History and theory—v. 2. Research methods—v. 3. Social structure—v. 4. Socialization—v. 5. Stratification and inequality—v. 6. Deviance and crime—v. 7. Social change.
  ISBN 978-0-8160-8314-5 (alk. paper)—ISBN 978-0-8160-8315-2 (v. 1 : alk. paper)—ISBN 978-0-8160-8316-9 (v. 2 : alk. paper)—ISBN 978-0-8160-8317-6 (v. 3 : alk. paper)—ISBN 978-0-8160-8319-0 (v. 4 : alk. paper)—ISBN 978-0-8160-8320-6 (v. 5 : alk. paper)—ISBN 978-0-8160-8321-3 (v. 6 : alk. paper)—ISBN 978-0-8160-8322-0 (v. 7 : alk. paper)
  1. Sociology. I. Grauerholz, Elizabeth, 1958–
  HM585.S796 2012
  301—dc23   2011025983

Facts On File books are available at special discounts when purchased in bulk quantities for businesses, associations, institutions, or sales promotions. Please call our Special Sales Department at (212) 967-8800 or (800) 322-8755.

You can find Facts On File on the World Wide Web at
http://www.infobaselearning.com

Text design and composition by Erika K. Arroyo
Cover printed by Yurchak Printing, Landisville, Pa.
Book printed and bound by Yurchak Printing, Landisville, Pa.
Date Printed: April 2012
Printed in the United States of America

10 9 8 7 6 5 4 3 2 1

This book is printed on acid-free paper.

CONTENTS

FOREWORD

The United States has the highest incarceration rate in the world! More than 3 percent of U.S. residents are in jails, prisons, or on parole. This number far exceeds those of other countries, including those we may consider to be far more "repressive" than the United States. Furthermore, the rate of incarceration has grown (along with the number of prisons) significantly over the past three decades. One conclusion you might draw from these statistics is that today's Americans are more deviant than ever and are committing more crimes than they had in the past. When viewed through a sociological lens, the true state of things is much more complex. The enormous growth in the prison population in our country is not necessarily due to more crime or a deviance-prone society. Instead, it is more likely a reflection of political, historical, economic, and other social factors that often go unrecognized.

The study of crime and deviance is one of the richest sociological areas of investigation. In this volume, you will learn how social forces converge to give rise to new ways of defining and dealing with crime and deviance. Here, you will learn about direct effects of policy and other sociolegal processes on individuals' lives and observe how changes in socialization practices, gender and racial inequality, and norms (among other things) shape acts of deviance and crime. In short, the study of crime and deviance will help you understand the world from a more sociological perspective.

Professor Muschert begins this volume with a profound observation—that although the sociology of crime and deviance may seem to concern the "abnormal, distasteful, immoral, and illegal," in reality it is a study of the most fundamental aspects of society and social life. You will learn that without deviance or crime, society as we know it would not exist—and not simply because we wouldn't be afraid of being victimized or have little to hear about on the news.

Rather, deviance and crime help a society define itself by allowing for better comprehension of what is important, of value, and worth fighting for. Without deviance and crime, it would not be so easy to determine appropriate behavior in public and with other people. Thus, studying deviance and crime also gives us a better understanding of our cultural values.

Of course, another reason to study crime and deviance is because both are features of our lives. Crime and deviance dominate the news. Many of us know people (perhaps even ourselves) who have been arrested and spent time in jail or prison. And it is probably safe to say that all of us have been deviant in one way or another, although we may not have been labeled as such. This volume will help put these experiences into a broader perspective. As you read, you will not only gain insight into society but you may also gain insight into yourself and others and how the experiences you have had with crime and deviance have been shaped by larger social forces such as race, gender, and age. Such is the promise of sociology.

—Liz Grauerholz, University of Central Florida

INTRODUCTION

This text differs from most other texts on a similar topic available on the market today. Most criminology texts are similar: They define crime, offer data and trends, outline theories of crime causation, and describe crime typologies. Deviance texts are of two types. The first is conceptually based and discusses the sociological principles behind deviancy. The second is a more descriptive approach that takes a laundry-list approach by describing various forms of deviance (e.g., sexuality, drugs, violence, etc.). This text is a hybrid of the conceptually based and the descriptive texts. Each chapter presents the underlying sociological concepts involved in understanding crime and/or deviance. From this text, you should take away both a conceptual understanding of principles in deviance/crime and a better understanding of the descriptive aspects of various forms of crime and deviance.

The strength to this hybrid approach is that you can get a sense of how sociologically to understand crime and deviance in general and, more specifically, see how both apply to concrete behaviors. In addition, you can garner a better factual understanding of real-world examples of criminal/deviant behaviors, many of which you may find intriguing. Most texts cover either crime or deviance, and perhaps with good reason. On the other hand, many deviance courses get conflated with criminology courses. In this text, I have taken up the challenge of presenting crime and deviance together. The potential weakness of the text is that you will fail to draw connections between the conceptual and applied examples offered here. This has been my job, one which I take on in partnership with your instructor.

In writing this text, I have pursued a number of worthy goals: My first goal is to introduce you to the sociological study of crime and deviance. For certain, each person has his or her own opinions about crime and deviant behaviors.

1

Each student may be exposed to varying degrees to crime and deviancy in the real world, and probably to a greater degree in news and entertainment media. However, it's also possible that you have not yet been exposed to the sociological study of these social phenomena. Thus, I have written a text that offers a comprehensive view of crime and deviancy studies. Above all, it is my hope to share my enthusiasm for this subject, and in so doing, to inspire you to develop your own sense of enthusiasm for the sociology of crime and deviance.

My second goal is to inspire you to increase your sociological literacy. Although each person has an awareness of the sociological landscape in which he or she lives, my goal is to help you become increasingly aware of the interplay between the choices that individuals make in their lives and the external factors or pressures that influence those choices. In so doing, our studies may help you to become aware of your own value judgments and those of others. Some factual explorations in the text may, at times, correct existing misconceptions, biases, myths, and stereotypes associated with deviance and crime as social phenomena. In turn, this new view on old concepts may help you to become more discriminating as judges of social behavior (both your own and that of others). Perhaps you will become more concerned about some forms of crime or deviance and less troubled by others.

My final goal has been to treat you as a junior colleague. Thank you for connecting with me through my words, and I am grateful that we are on this journey together to explore the sociological facets of criminal and deviant behaviors in society.

CHAPTER 1

THE SOCIOLOGY OF CRIME AND DEVIANCE: A LOOK INTO THE BASIC ISSUES OF SOCIAL LIFE

Although the sociology of crime and deviance might at first sound like the study of the abnormal, distasteful, immoral, and illegal, it is in fact the study of central issues fundamental to social life. Indeed, the study of crime and deviance is an important part of the study of society as a whole. Simply defined, crime and deviance are violations of social norms, yet a deeper examination reveals that these are complicated issues. Much of the focus of deviance studies and criminology tends to be on the margins between acceptable and unacceptable behavior; that is, the heart of the matter is to examine the boundaries between right and wrong, between the acceptable and the unacceptable, and between insiders and outsiders.

This is a text about the social scientific study of social rules—their maintenance, enforcement, and transgression. It examines how rules are defined (and by whom), how they are maintained, and how they may be subject to change. It focuses both on informal processes and formal rituals in which rules are interpreted and applied; it focuses on enforcement of rules and responses to rule transgression; and finally, it examines the characteristics of social environments where norms are typically transgressed.

At the basis of the sociology of crime and deviance lie certain key issues, namely how the rules of social behavior are formed, maintained, and applied. Ironically, in the absence of deviance and crime, one observes conformity and legitimacy, factors which for most people in their day to day lives are unspoken and nonproblematic. However, the student of crime and deviance must examine

3

both the normal and the abnormal; the tasteful and the distasteful; the moral and the immoral; and the legal and illegal. In the examination of these aspects of human behavior, the student is invited on a journey into the sociology of crime and deviance, a fundamental examination of social life.

NORMS: THE RULES OF SOCIAL LIFE

Norms are among the most basic of concepts in the social sciences. **Norms** are the rules of social behavior, which define appropriate behavior in social interactions. In every situation, individuals look to social guidelines for behavior as a way of understanding which behaviors are desirable and which are undesirable. People are not born with an innate knowledge about the rules of social behavior; they learn the normative expectations of behavior in the process of living.

There are two general types of norms: prescriptive and proscriptive. **Prescriptive norms** are those rules of social behavior that describe the actions that are appropriate in social interactions. Just as a medical practitioner might advise that a patient take a medicine or undertake therapy, prescriptive norms tell us which behaviors are appropriate in social life. For example, when answering a telephone call, it is expected that the person receiving the call would offer a greeting such as "hello." Similarly, when working for a wage, the worker is expected to report the income to the proper authorities and to pay taxes on that

Formal dinner by the Washington Board of Trade for the governors of the states in 1908. Folkway norms can define and dictate table manners, conversation, and dress at such events. *(Library of Congress)*

income. Therefore, the prescriptive norms of offering a greeting when answering the phone and reporting taxable income both outline actions that should be taken as part of acceptable social behavior. On the other hand, **proscriptive norms** are those rules of social behavior that describe actions that are inappropriate. For example, it is considered impolite to talk with one's mouth full, and it is considered immoral to engage in sexual relations with one's immediate family members. Therefore, social norms clearly define that a person should not talk with a full mouth or commit incest. In short, we recognize that there are two varieties of norms: prescriptive norms that define what people are appropriately supposed to do, and proscriptive norms which define what people are not supposed to do.

In his 1906 book *Folkways*, Yale sociologist William Graham Sumner described three other categories of norms: folkways, mores, and laws. **Folkways** are those norms that describe the rules of polite behavior or etiquette. Folkway norms define all sorts of unspoken, yet clearly recognized norms such as table manners, how to interact with others in conversation, and how to dress. Violations of folkway norms are typically considered poor taste. For example, in Western cultures, it is customary to shake hands as a greeting when meeting someone; in East Asian cultures, it is customary to bow as a greeting. The failure to offer the appropriate greeting is interpreted as rudeness.

Another common folkway is that many recognize an imaginary line between two people engaged in conversation and try to avoid walking through that line. As an experiment you might try the following: Maintain a wider than average distance while standing with another person in a hallway or other walkway. Engage in a conversation and observe how many others will avoid walking through the "conversation line." In some cases they will bend down to avoid breaking the imaginary line. Those who can avoid walking between the two persons are likely to do so; those who do walk in between or break the line will often excuse themselves. This experiment can help illus-

Seinfeld: A Television Show About Folkways

Much of the well-known TV show *Seinfeld* centers on the humorous situations that ensue when characters violate the normal expectations of polite behavior. For example, consider some of the recognizable situations from the show: standing too close to other people when talking to them, characters eating a candy bar with a knife and fork, a soup vendor who verbally abuses his customers and refuses to sell them his product, sleeping under one's desk while at work, claiming that one has a job at a fictional company, and preparing food in one's shower. These and many other examples from the show illustrate folkway-type norms and their violation.

trate the existence of a subtle, yet widely recognized, folkway about communicative behavior.

Mores (pronounced *mohr'- eyz*) are norms that refer to moral rules for behavior. Moral expectations for behavior may be religious in nature, although many pluralistic societies also maintain secular notions for what is considered ethical. Actions that violate more-type norms are considered sinful or unethical. For example, most cultures maintain a strict moral and ethical prohibition of incest, and thus incestuous relations are considered morally wrong.

Laws, the third type of norms, are the formally written and codified rules of a society or group. Legal boundaries for behavior come in two varieties: civil and criminal. **Civil laws** regulate relationships between individuals and are designed to protect the private interests of citizens or groups. For example, if a person's negligence causes damage to another person's property, the aggrieved party can sue via the civil law for repair or replacement of the damaged property. **Criminal laws** regulate the behavior of all citizens and are designed to protect the interests of the entire society. For example, if a person commits a violent offense such as rape, the interest of the entire society to maintain peace is threatened (not just the peacefulness of the victim). Therefore, most societies maintain formal mechanisms for justice, including arrest, judgment, and punishment of offenders. The violation of a criminal law is known as a **crime**, and as a subarea within the sociology of deviance, **criminology** is the study of social behavior associated with violations of criminal laws.

Important Distinctions Concerning Crimes

By legal definition, there are two necessary elements for an action to be considered a crime. First, there must be criminal intent or ***mens rea*** (Latin, meaning *guilty mind*), which means that the offender must show malice aforethought. A commonly cited Latin expression that captures the concept is *actus non facit reum nisi mens sit rea*, which means "the act does not make a person guilty unless the mind is also guilty." Most commonly, the standard for establishing *mens rea* is that a person must purposefully and knowingly undertake a criminal action; otherwise it is not considered a crime. This means that intentionality is a crucial factor in determining whether a crime has occurred, although there are factors which can mitigate responsibility.

The second necessary element for an action to be considered a crime is ***actus reus*** (Latin, meaning *guilty act*), which means that by definition a crime requires that an illegal act must have taken place. There are three ways that *actus reus* may be established: by commission, when an action has taken place; by omission, when a required action has not taken place; and by possession, which refers to inappropriate possession of objects or materials. Thus, merely thinking about committing a crime is not in itself illegal, nor is holding unorthodox beliefs or attitudes, nor is being in an undesirable state (such as drug addiction).

What About the Insanity Plea?

Psychologists undoubtedly assert that many convicted offenders have mental health issues such as depression, antisocial personality disorder, and addictions. Because of this, the question arises whether offenders with psychological conditions should be considered insane. The psychological and legal definitions of insanity, however, vary greatly. From a psychological point of view, most offenders with mental disorders are considered worthy of psychiatric treatment, but they are held legally responsible for their actions. In the legal sense, individuals are considered insane only if they suffer from a mental condition that fundamentally skews their perception of reality (e.g., if they significantly hallucinate or hear voices) or if they are incapable of understanding the consequences of their actions (e.g., if their sense of cause and effect is impaired). Some defendants who are legally insane receive the disposition "guilty but mentally ill," in which case they serve part of their sentence in a mental hospital and the rest of the sentence in a typical prison setting.

Among criminal laws, there are two varieties of actions **mala in se** (Latin, meaning *wrong in itself*) and **mala prohibitium** (Latin, meaning *wrong as prohibited*). *Mala in se* refers to those actions that are considered illegal because they are inherently wrong. Most societies consider a number of behaviors to be inherently wrong (e.g., murder, rape, stealing, and lying) or even taboo (e.g., incest and pedophilia). Thus, behaviors considered *mala in se* are not prohibited simply because they violate the standards of the particular social group making the laws, but rather because they are considered essentially wrong.

Who Is Not Responsible?

The establishment of criminal intent (*mens rea*) is an important factor in determining whether a crime has occurred. However, even if people commit acts that are normally considered illegal, those who cannot form criminal intent cannot be held criminally responsible because they do not meet the legal standard for *mens rea*. The following categories of persons often are incapable of fully forming criminal intent: children (especially those under the age of 12); those suffering from mental conditions involving hallucinations or psychosis; and those with developmental disabilities (which limit their capacity for intellectual and/or moral reasoning). Being under the influence of alcohol or drugs, although these substances might cause impairment, is not a legally valid reason to waive criminal intent.

In comparison, ***mala prohibitium*** refers to those behaviors considered illegal because they are determined within the social group to be wrong. For example, legal standards vary from jurisdiction to jurisdiction regarding behaviors such as gambling, consumption of controlled substances, and prostitution. While these behaviors might be prohibited in some states or countries, they will be allowed by law in other states or countries. Thus, behaviors considered *mala prohibitium* are prohibited because they violate the standards of the group making the laws, not because they are intrinsically wrong.

The Relationship Between Crime and Deviance

Deviance is defined as the transgression of one or more social norms of various types, including folkways, mores, and laws. Crime is defined more narrowly as the violation of one or more criminal laws. Given this, what is the relationship between deviance and crime? Basically, the categories are overlapping, but they do diverge. Deviance is a broader category in that it encompasses behaviors that violate any social norms. There is, however, a large area that fits under the rubric of social deviance that is not considered criminal. For example, violations of folkways, such as dressing inappropriately, displaying poor etiquette, or speaking rudely to one's family members are all considered deviant, but not criminal. Similarly, actions that violate moral codes, such as sex outside of marriage and lying to one's family members, are likewise considered deviant but not criminal.

On the other hand, there are areas of strong overlap between the concepts of crime and deviance. Crime is defined as the violation of criminal laws, and laws are a variety of norms. Thus, most crimes are also deviant. For example, use of illegal drugs, illegal gambling, and illicit prostitution are both criminal and deviant, because these actions violate criminal laws. What clouds the issue is that many mores and laws overlap, as the legal code often reflects the general moral sentiment. For example, murder, rape, and theft are both deviant and criminal, because these actions are prohibited both by moral codes and by laws.

Sections above described how deviance and crime are likely to overlap. Here the focus is on criminal behavior that may or may not by considered deviant or deviant behavior that may or may not be considered criminal. Some people, for example, engage in behaviors that are considered illegal but are commonly practiced. One specific example of this is cheating on taxes, behavior that is legally prohibited but may be commonly practiced. Those in service positions, such as restaurant servers or bartenders, may as a routine course of their jobs underreport tip income. An even more common example is the many motorists who routinely exceed the speed limit. As long as they are not cited by traffic police for what is illegal behavior, most do not feel as if they have violated a social norm.

Along the same lines, there are behaviors which are morally reprehensible, but which are not prohibited by law. For example, in the United States, a person is not legally obligated to help another, such as a drowning person, someone who has been in an accident, or someone who is choking. Although it seems ethically clear that a person should help another person as long as such help does not put the helper in harm's way, there is no legal obligation to do so. Allowing another person to drown or choke to death clearly violates the moral sensibility but is not a violation of law and is therefore not a crime.

Social Control as Response to Deviance

Norms set the behavioral foundations for social life whereas deviance transgresses those social norms. Actions designed to enforce social norms and to regulate behavior are known as **social control**. Control mechanisms vary widely, from mild expressions of disapproval to capital punishment, although all are intended to respond to the transgression of norms. One distinction in types of social control is between internal and external forms. **Internal social control** refers to mechanisms within an individual that regulate behavior, as when a person may integrate social norms into a personal sense of conscience and in so doing develop means to self-regulate behavior. This sort of self-control is an internalization of the social expectations for behavior and indicates the normal socialization of the individual into the social environment. Internal control mechanisms operate both on the rational level (e.g., when people weigh their actions and their potential consequences) and on the emotional level (e.g., when people are adverse to behaviors because they find them abhorrent). For example, most people find the idea of abusing a child or an animal repugnant, and although adults can usually outsmart and/or overpower children and animals, most nonetheless abhor their mistreatment.

External social control refers to any method outside the individual which regulates behavior. When violating social norms, individuals may be criticized or sanctioned by others, and these social responses are external forms of control. The response (i.e., the control) may be formal or informal.

Informal social control refers to the "unceremonious" responses from others—that is, responses that are likely to be personal, implicit, or unofficial in nature. Informal control seems to be a stronger feature of tradition-oriented societies, which rely more strongly on customary social practices to regulate behavior. Informal mechanisms include disapproval, criticism, ridicule, and shaming. At more extreme levels, discrimination, ostracism, and shunning may be exercised against those violating norms. For example, many pre-modern societies may shun members who violate fundamental norms, and such shunning causes a social death of the person violating the norms.

Formal social control refers to the responses to deviance undertaken by government agents and formal organizations, whose responses are described in laws or policies. Such responses tend to be impersonal, explicit, and ceremonious in nature. For example, the police (as formal agents of social control) may arrest someone accused of committing a crime. The arrest may lead to

Child sitting in a corner. Ostracism is a form of informal social control. *(Carl Larsson. Wikipedia)*

a formal trial, followed by an officially mandated punishment. Formal social control seems to be a dominant feature in modern and heterogeneous societies, which cannot rely on custom or tradition to regulate social behavior. Formal control is performed by official agencies (such as government agents or police) who may apply such sanctions as fines and imprisonment.

APPLYING CONCEPTS OF DEVIANCE TO GENDER AND SEXUALITY

In any society, gender, sexuality, and sexual behavior are among the most highly scrutinized subjects, often generating significant public attention. Although issues of sexuality and gender may seem like personal topics that should remain private and outside of the influence of the social realm, these subject are in fact quite public and subject to social definition and scrutiny. On all levels (including folkways, moral codes, and laws) sexuality and gender are subject to social definition, as societies define what behaviors fall inside and outside the boundaries of propriety in sexual behaviors and gender relations. When transgressed, the norms regulating gender expectations and sexual behaviors can spark intense social control responses. As such, gender and sexuality provide a fascinating study into how deviance operates in society.

Human beings are sexual beings by nature, though these innate tendencies are regulated by social norms, quite often in the form of moral codes. An examination of norms governing sexual behaviors is somewhat complicated because these behaviors cut across two distinct, yet overlapping sociological categories: sex and gender. **Sex** refers to the physiological characteristics of the person, i.e., whether a person is male or female. A person's male or female status is recognized as a legal status by the state. In contrast, **gender** is a social category that refers to the roles, attributes, expectations, and behaviors which are accepted for men and women, most commonly in the form of social norms of masculinity and femininity.

Typically, sex and gender correspond to one another, in that persons who are sexually male behave within the boundaries of masculine gender roles, while those who are female conduct themselves according to feminine roles. Indeed, for most people gender and sexual identities are fixed categories, meaning that they do not change during the life course. However, this is not always the case, and for a minority of persons, gender and sexuality may change over time. For example, it is possible for a person to pursue hormone treatments and sex reassignment surgery, if that person prefers to change sex from male to female or vice versa. Those who are pursuing, or who have completed sex-change procedures are known as **transsexual**. Some states allow persons to change their legal sex, if they have sex reassignment surgery; other states prohibit the change. Conceptually distinct are people who choose to retain their sex but change their social behaviors to conform to the other gender's social expectations. Such individuals are known as **transgender**. For example, it is possible for a person who is physiologically male to live socially in a feminine role, or vice versa, a status known as **cross-dressing**. Such persons typically derive no sexual pleasure from cross-dressing, but are instead motivated by the emotional satisfaction they derive from living socially as the other gender.

Sexual orientation is a term that refers to a person's tendency to develop romantic feelings and sexual attraction toward a specific sex/gender. **Heterosexuality**, or straight orientation, is most common in our culture—men are attracted to women and vice versa. However, other sexual orientations are observed in our culture, including **homosexuality**, which is the attraction to the members of the same sex. Specifically, gay men are attracted to other men, and lesbian women are attracted to other women. **Sexual identity** is a term that refers to how a person describes his or her sexuality, including how that person relates to others. The concept of sexual identity touches upon issues related both to sexual preference and to gender performance. The acceptance of same-sex relationships and persons is at times a hotly contested issue as some subcultures and moral codes prohibit same-sex relations. Mainstream society generally condones heterosexual preference and relationships as the norm, something known as **heteronormativity**. In recent decades, there has been significant activity on the part of social movements to provide gay men and lesbians with the same legal and social status afforded to straight persons.

Thinking about sexuality and gender is dominated by a number of binary concepts in oppositions, including male/female, man/woman, and straight/gay. Although these categories dominate the awareness of sex and gender, there are a number of other categories that do not fit within these binary opposites. With regards to physical sex, a small percentage of people are born with chromosomes, genitalia, or secondary sex traits associated with males and females, a medical term known as **intersex**. Alternately, some individuals do not feel strongly aligned with either the masculine or feminine gender roles, and therefore may be termed as gender queer (meaning they do not conform to either gender) or androgynous (meaning their gender performance is ambiguously between masculine and feminine roles). An example is the case of the third gender category called *hijra* (observed in India and Pakistan) in which a biological male lives according to a feminine gender identity, or the Native American concept of Two-Spirit, in which a person may identify as having a masculine and feminine spirit within one body. Finally, with regards to sexual orientation and identity, some persons do not align with either hetero- or same-sex expression. For example, bisexual persons are attracted to both men and women and often maintain a distinctly different sexual identity (i.e., neither gay nor straight nor

Participants carry a rainbow flag during the Marcha Gay in Mexico City. *(Wikipedia. Courtesy of Thelmadatter)*

somewhere in between). Alternately, individuals may practice celibacy, which is the suppression of any sexual expression, commonly (but not exclusively) practiced by people in religious communities.

Norms governing sex and gender vary from the most informal of social practices to serious moral codes and legal prescriptions. In addition, the violation of these norms often may spark intense social control responses. Often in subtle ways, notions of sex and gender expectations for social behavior pervade folkway norms regulating the informal, polite sense of how people should interact. For example, there are informal expectations that males typically should conform to masculine roles and that females should conform to feminine roles. Those who do not conform may risk criticism or ostracism by others, which is to say that the violation of gender norms can evoke a strong social control response. On a more mundane level an example of a folkway norm about gender is that boys are taught not to hit girls under any circumstances, while hitting other boys may sometimes be acceptable. Those boys who hit girls may be subject to intense disapproval or other punishments.

Aspects of sex and gender also pervade moral sensibilities, as moral codes often regulate the circumstances in which it is appropriate to engage in sexual relations with others and who appropriate partners might be. For example, many religious traditions stipulate that sexual relations should only occur within the confines of marriage between one man and one woman. This moral understanding then prohibits a variety of sexual relations including the following: masturbation, premarital sex, extramarital sex, same-sex relations, and sex with multiple partners. Although we observe no legal prohibitions for these sexual relations prohibited by religious traditions, those who engage in these behaviors may be judged negatively. Of course, there are other moral sensibilities besides

Prurient Pursuits

Behaviors that are unusual or shocking often garner attention, especially those behaviors that involve sexual expression. In the discussion of sex, much focus falls upon prurient pursuits, such as fetishes or consumption of pornography. Fetishism refers to the sexual arousal a person derives from focusing on a certain body part or attribute, whereas paraphilia refers to sexual arousal derived from inanimate objects. For example, transvestites might derive sexual pleasure from dressing in clothing associated with the opposite gender. Pornography involves the depiction of explicit sexual material for the purposes of titillation. Porn of some form is legal in most locations, though depictions of hardcore or extreme pornographic acts are often considered obscene. Consumption of porn is commonly opposed by many religious groups and groups supporting women's rights.

Sodomy Laws

Sodomy is a term that refers to penile-anal sex, often between two men. In the past, sodomy had been prohibited under state laws, as it was considered an unnatural sex act. Since anal sex has often been associated with sex between gay men, critics argued that sodomy laws discriminated against gay men. As of 2002, 36 states had repealed their antisodomy laws, and in 2003 the U.S. Supreme Court invalidated all remaining state sodomy laws. The decision arose from the following case. In 1998, two gay men in Texas were engaged in consensual intercourse, when a law enforcement office entered their residence after receiving a false report of a disturbance. The two men were arrested, charged, and convicted of sodomy. Gay rights legal defense teams appealed the case, which ultimately ended up on the U.S. Supreme Court docket in the 2003 case *Lawrence v. Texas*. The court decided that sodomy laws were in fact discriminatory against gays, because they violated an adults' rights to privacy in their consensual sex acts. Although some moral and religious sensibilities still prohibit sodomy, the Supreme Court decision in *Lawrence v. Texas* means that consensual sexual acts between adults are no longer legally prohibited, regardless of the sexual orientation of those engaging in those acts.

those in religious traditions, so one can also find groups that positively condone a wide variety of sexual relations.

Variation in moral sensibility reflects the pluralistic character of contemporary society. For example, some in religious traditions might condemn same-sex relations, while those who live in or tolerate same-sex relations disagree. Thus, the issue of gay rights becomes an issue within a culture, a war between traditionalist mindsets and more progressive mindsets. This has led to the rise of a social movement group sometimes called **LGBTQ**, which stands for "Lesbian, Gay, Bisexual, Transgender, and Questioning/Queer." This group is a coalition among those whose sexual orientation, sexual identity, or gender does not conform to traditional standards, and thus LGBTQ groups advocate for social and civil liberties for those who fit LGBTQ definitions.

Finally, the state also regulates sexuality and gender in the form of laws. For example, the state records a person's physiological sex and regulates the minimum age at which one may consent to sexual relations. In recent years, there has been consistent political discussion regarding legal issues related to sexual identity and gender. For example, there is a dispute over whether openly same-sex oriented persons should be allowed to serve in the military. Traditionally, gays and lesbians were excluded from military service, because homosexuality was at that time defined as a psychological infirmity. In 1993, the military began practicing a policy known as "Don't Ask, Don't Tell," which meant that a

Kai Erikson's *Wayward Puritans*

In *Wayward Puritans*, sociologist Kai Erikson examined the social functions of deviance, focusing on 17th century Puritan society in the Massachusetts Bay Colony. Erikson argued that the violation of norms and the confrontation between norm violators and agents of social control helped to reinforce the moral sentiment within the society at large. He suggested that deviance was necessary because it helped to maintain the boundaries of the group, which were defined by behaviors, either permitted or prohibited. Unless some persons transgressed the rules, the bounds of acceptable behavior would not be clear to society as a whole. Therefore, both deviant behavior and the responses to deviant behavior are necessary for the healthy functioning of any social group, because they reaffirm the norms and increase group conformity and solidarity. Each social group must maintain its characteristic forms of deviance, which will persist over time due to their useful role in redefining the norms and solidarity of that particular group. Erikson concentrated especially on the varieties of deviance and social control observed in Puritan society, specifically those related to witch trials. Although our common conception of the Puritans was that they were a highly controlled society, at the time of the witch scares the Puritans were experiencing times of rapid social change and uncertainty. Erikson argued that the witch trials allowed Puritan society to unite around a common enemy, the threat posed by witches, and therefore to maintain greater conformity and cohesion within the group.

Puritan witch trial *(Joseph E. Baker. Wikipedia)*

person's sexual orientation was considered private and should not be asked about or disclosed. In effect, this policy meant that gay or lesbian persons could serve in the military as long as they were not open about their sexual orientation. Effective in 2011, the "Don't Ask, Don't Tell" policy was repealed, allowing openly gay persons to serve in the military.

Another related culture war—related to gay marriage—has occurred over the past decade, and this issue is one of law because states legally regulate marriage relationships. Traditionally, the legal concept has been that a marriage is a relationship between one man and one woman. However, LGBTQ groups and their allies have argued that excluding gay persons from the right to marry is discriminatory because it excludes them from receiving benefits afforded to heterosexual couples, such as insurance benefits, inheritance benefits, retirement benefits, and the positive social sanctioning of the relationship by the state. At present, some states allow gay unions while other states prohibit gay unions, even to the point of refusing to recognize gay unions legally performed in other states. The issue of gay marriage is fundamentally tied to both legal and moral senses of which intimate/family relationships should be endorsed by the society at large.

SUMMARY

As a subfield of sociology, the examination of deviance and crime is fundamental to the study of all social life, from the most insignificant practices of etiquette to the broadest dialogue about social issues. Potentially, some of the topics discussed in this text may be new, bizarre, or even offensive to some readers. It is important to understand that each person has an internal moral compass (known as a conscience), which means that individuals rarely approach the study of crime and deviance with pure objectivity. Even so, it is also important to grapple with different and potentially troubling ideas, because it is often on these margins that the most significant learning occurs. Unfortunately, attempts to understand seemingly strange behaviors are often mistaken as efforts to justify those behaviors. This text attempts to help the student to understand a variety of deviant behaviors, and it is important to clarify that students may certainly retain their inherent right to judge the appropriateness of any behavior for themselves. Remember that the goal here is to promote an understanding of deviant and criminal behaviors, not to convince you of the rightness or wrongness of actions. The assumption is that knowing about the multiplicity of human life, with its myriad dynamics, is much better that hiding one's head in the sand.

Further Reading

Chasnoff, Deborah (producer). *Straightlaced: How Gender's Got Us All Tied Up*. Groundspark Films, 2006.

Erikson, Kai. *Wayward Puritans: A Study in the Sociology of Deviance*. New York: Allyn & Bacon, 2004.

Everyday Sociology Blog. Available at http://nortonbooks.typepad.com/everydaysociology/trends/.

Heckert, Alex, and Druann Maria Heckert. "An Integrated Typology of Deviance Applied to Ten Middle Class Norms." *Sociological Quarterly* 45 (2004): 209–228.

Marx, Gary T. "Ironies of Social Control: Authorities as Contributors to Deviance through Escalation, Nonenforcement and Covert Facilitation." 1974. Chapter available electronically at http://web.mit.edu/gtmarx/www/ironies.html.

Pfohl, Stephen. "The 'Discovery' of Child Abuse." *Social Problems* 24 (1977): 310–323.

Scott, Robert A. *The Making of Blind Men*. New York: Transaction Publishers, 1981.

CHAPTER 2

MEASURING CRIME RATES AND TRENDS

As a subset of deviant behaviors, crimes attract a lot of attention, both from the public at large and from professionals charged with responding to criminal acts. Two of the biggest challenges are to understand the types of crimes taking place and to collect accurate information about how many crimes are occurring. To maintain accurate crime statistics, a number of methods are utilized.

Perhaps the most frequently cited crime statistics are derived from the **Uniform Crime Reports** (commonly known as UCRs), standardized reporting forms created by the Federal Bureau of Investigation (FBI) in 1930 to collect data on criminal events across the country. This form is now used by police officers across the country to record the basic details of every criminal event reported to the police, including information about the type of offense and information about both the offender and victim (if any), including age, sex, and race/ethnicity. Today, approximately 17,000 law enforcement agencies in the United States, serving approximately 90 percent of the population, participate in UCR reporting. The FBI tracks a variety of crimes, including violent crimes and property crimes. When citing crime statistics, most people in law enforcement today refer to what are called the Part I crimes, which comprise four violent crimes (i.e., murder, rape, assault, and robbery) and four property crimes (i.e., burglary, larceny, motor vehicle theft, and arson).

In 1960, a supplemental form called the **National Incident-Based Reporting System Supplement** to the UCRs (known as NIBRS, and commonly pronounced as *nigh-buhrs*) was developed. NIBRS allows police to report a

Police officer takes notes. *(Library of Congress)*

greater level of detail about criminal events, including a detailed description of the event, the offenders, victims (if any), value of property damaged/stolen (if any), and the description of the person(s) arrested for the crime. Together, the UCR and NIBRS reports are the primary large-scale source of data about criminal events available in the United States. Each year, the FBI releases a report of crime in the United States, and these are available to the public. (See the Further Reading listed at the end of this chapter for an Internet link to the report.)

The other major source of national-level data about criminal events is known as the **National Crime Victimization Survey** (NCVS), which since 1973 has collected information from households in the United States regarding crime victimization experienced by those living in the home. The NCVS is administered by the U.S. Census Bureau on behalf of the Bureau of Justice Statistics twice per year via a random telephone survey of approximately 49,000 U.S. households, which include about 100,000 persons. Like the UCRs, the NCVS asks respondents to describe the characteristics of any criminal events in which they were victims, including the nature of the event, the description of the offenders and victims, the value of property damaged/stolen (if any), and the details of those arrested in connection to the crime. The NCVS measures the same varieties of crimes measured by the UCR data, with the obvious exception of murder because murder victims cannot respond to surveys.

Other Methods of Studying Crimes

Although the UCR and NCVS data are among the most-cited forms of information about crime rates, criminologists in fact employ a wide variety of methods to study crime. Some studies directly ask a group to self-report their criminal activities, as in cases where youth are asked to identify their pattern of drug use. Alternately, sociologists sometimes spend time living with and observing a group they want to study. For example, to learn about a drug smuggling ring or a street gang, a sociologist might live with the group. In other cases, criminologists might interview people about their criminal offense(s) or victimization, often in return for a small monetary reward.

A fundamental difference between the UCR and the NCVS is that the former documents information gathered and compiled by police and the latter records information directly from victims of a crime. These are two different phenomena, and the NCVS tends to suggest a higher rate of crime than that recorded in the UCRs. It is worth noting, however, that the UCR and NCVS data frequently show similar trends in rates of offense/victimization. When the rate of victimization reported in the NCVS changes, we tend also to observe a proportionate change in UCR data. These corroborated trends in crime rates reported in multiple data sets are significant: Although we may not be entirely confident that we are capturing the true number of crimes occurring, we are reasonably confident that we are accurately noting the trends—that is, whether the number of crimes of a particular kind are increasing, holding steady, or declining.

It is worth noting that all data about crime are limited, and by virtue of these limitations, inherently imperfect. There are systematic reasons why crime statistics are limited, many of which are unavoidable. To begin with, a victim may be unaware that a crime has taken place (e.g., when something is stolen but the victim doesn't notice it is gone). Sometimes, in fact, a victim does not even know that a particular event is considered a crime (as in the case of children or persons with developmental disability who are unaware they are being victimized). Another limiting factor is that a crime may be unreported. Rape victims, for example, sometimes choose to keep their victimization hidden and private. Other crime victims simply believe that the process of reporting a crime is too complicated, especially if an incident involved only a petty crime. Finally, some crimes may be reported but go unrecorded, as in cases when police are notified but an officer may choose not to fill out the appropriate paperwork about the event. These limitations to accurate and complete crime data point toward what is known as the **dark figure of crime**, which refers to the discrepancy

John Conklin's *Why Crime Rates Fell*

By the early 1990s, America had experienced a decade of declining crime rates. Criminologists were struggling to understand what was causing this change, while politicians and police were lining up to take credit for the decline. In 2003, criminologist John Conklin attempted to explain why crime rates were on the decline. The book starts with an in-depth discussion of how data about crimes are collected and compiled, and then turns to a discussion of small policy changes that police agencies (most notably the New York Police Dept.) had made. Specifically, police in New York started more aggressively ticketing for minor infractions, such as jumping over the subway turnstile and jaywalking. The police claimed that this led to a heightened sense among the population that even minor infractions would not be tolerated, much less more serious infractions. Conklin suggests that the decline in crimes of all types observed since the early 1990s may be an interaction between changes in police tactics and other factors that are unrelated to police activity. For example, during this period, the economic outlook in the United States improved greatly and crack cocaine was no longer the blight in urban areas it once had been. In addition, the proportion of those who would be in their prime crime-committing years (i.e., young males, 18 to 24 years of age), comprised a smaller proportion of the population. As a whole, the book gives an overview of the multiple factors that may have contributed to declining crime rates since the early 1990s.

between how much crime actually exists and how much crime criminologists are apprised of. But despite the limitations of UCR and NCVS data, they are the best, most reliable sources of information about crimes occurring in the United States, and they are of great help in describing the extent of criminal activity and crime trends in this country.

TRENDS IN CRIME

In the last two decades, most U.S. localities and states (including rural, suburban, and urban areas) have experienced a significant and sustained period of decline in rates of criminal offense. This well-documented decline has at times mystified social scientists. At the same time, most people don't even know a decline in crime rates has occurred; some are even convinced that crime rates are increasing. One reason for this is that people continue to hear about shocking and horrible crimes in news media reports and therefore assume that the crime problem is intensifying. Fortunately, reliable UCR and NCVS data indicate that we currently live in a time when crime rates are at their lowest in forty years.

As noted above, the FBI tracks **violent crimes** (which are crimes against persons involving force, intimidation, coercion, or deception) and **property**

Crime Rates

In 2009, there were 1,318,398 violent crimes reported, however one rarely sees such information, because crimes are more frequently described in terms of their rates of occurrence per 100,000 persons in the population. Thus, the U.S. violent crime rate for 2009 would be computed as follows: the number of violent crimes reported divided by the population for that year, times 100,000. That is, 1,318,398 ÷ 307,006,550 × 100,000 = 429.4. Therefore, in 2009, the U.S. violent crime rate was 429.4 violent crimes per 100,000 persons in the population. The advantage of using crime rates is that they offer a consistent basis for comparison across years or between geographic areas, specifically because they control for fluctuations in the population.

crimes (which are crimes involving the destruction, misuse, or theft of items of value). The UCR data indicate that in 2009, there were 1,318,398 violent crimes and 9,320,971 property crimes reported in the United States. These raw numbers may seem shockingly high, but when you consider that the U.S. population

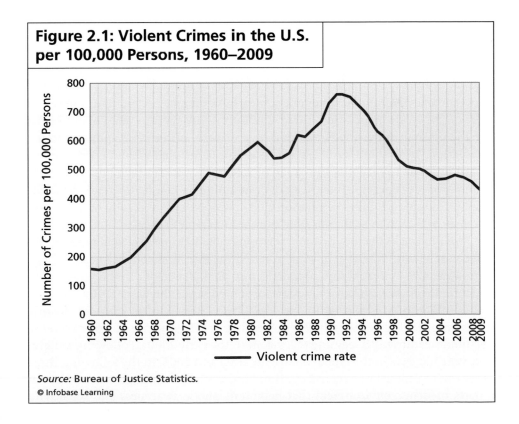

Figure 2.1: Violent Crimes in the U.S. per 100,000 Persons, 1960–2009

Violent crime rate

Source: Bureau of Justice Statistics.

© Infobase Learning

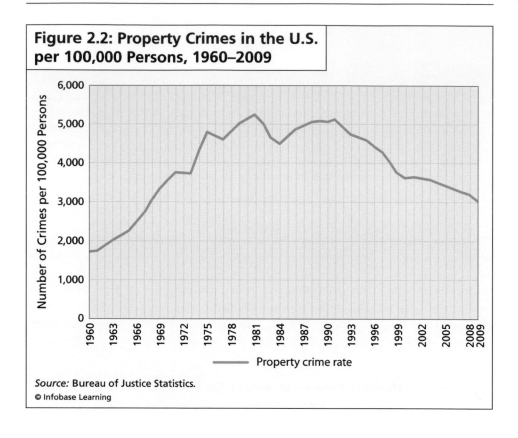

Figure 2.2: Property Crimes in the U.S. per 100,000 Persons, 1960–2009

Property crime rate

Source: Bureau of Justice Statistics.
© Infobase Learning

that year was 307,006,550, you get a somewhat different perspective. Viewed in light of the entire population, these numbers translate into one violent crime per 232 persons in the population and one property crime per 33 persons in the population. With these numbers, it is possible to see that violent crimes are in fact only about 8 percent of the crime problem; the remaining 92 percent comprise various property crimes. Clearly, raw numbers can be unwieldy and difficult to interpret. It is for this reason that criminologists typically refer to rates of crime, rather than to the absolute number of crimes reported.

The FBI tracks the four primary forms of violent crime (murder, rape, aggravated assault, and robbery) in what is called the **Part I violent crimes**. In 2009, there were 429.4 violent crimes reported per 100,000 persons in the population, which is the lowest violent crime rate observed since the early 1970s, as illustrated in Figure 2.1. Starting in the 1960s, the rate of violent offenses steadily increased, peaking in the early 1990s. Starting in 1993, the rate of violent offense declined steadily, until seeming to level off in the early 2000s. Following a slight, two-year increase in the rate of offense in 2005 and 2006, in the following three years the violent crime rate has continued to decline. Although we may live in a mass mediated environment that heightens public awareness and sensitivity to violent crime as a social issue, the data indicate that we are indeed living in a relatively safe time.

The FBI also monitors four primary forms of property crime, namely larceny-theft, burglary, motor vehicle theft, and arson, in what is called the **Part I property crimes**. These property index crimes are the focus of a section in the following chapter. In 2009, there were 3036.1 property crimes reported per 100,000 persons in the population, which is the lowest property crime rate observed since the late 1960s, as illustrated in Figure 2.2. In the 1960s, property crime began rising steadily over a number of years until stabilizing at a relatively high level from 1975 until about 1991. Starting in the early 1990s, property crimes began a steady decline until reaching the present level.

The trends for both violent crime and property crime rates have followed the same general pattern of rising since the early 1960s, and then declining again in the early 1990s until reaching the present levels. However, there are some differences in the trends between these two general categories of crimes. In the mid-1970s, the property crime rate leveled off, while the violent crime rate continued to climb until 1991. In addition, the property crime rate at its highest reached almost triple its 1960 level, while the violent crime rate ultimately reached almost five times its 1960 level.

Part I Violent Crimes

In all, violent crimes make up about 8 percent of the total crime problem in any given year. Assaults and robberies account for the vast majority of violent crimes reported to police, whereas murders and rapes are comparatively less frequent. The trends in the four types of events constituting Part I violent crimes generally follow the trend in the index as a whole, as illustrated in Figure 2.3. This section examines each of the violent index crimes individually.

Murder and Manslaughter

Murder, also known as **homicide**, is the unlawful killing of another person with malice aforethought. This means that to be responsible for murder, an offender must have thought about the consequences of the crime, no matter how briefly, before killing another person. **Non-negligent manslaughter** (also called **voluntary manslaughter**) is the unlawful killing of another person in the heat of the moment or in a sudden argument. The person committing this crime does intend to harm the victim, but that harm is not premeditated. Although not a Part I crime, **involuntary manslaughter**, should be mentioned here for contrastive purposes. This form of manslaughter occurs when a person has acted in a manner that clearly indicates disregard for the harm his or her actions might inflict on another, for example, a drunken motorist who kills another person in a vehicular accident.

The murder rate peaked in 1991 (at 9.8 per 100,000), at which point it steadily declined to its present level (at 5.0 per 100,000 in 2009). As the most

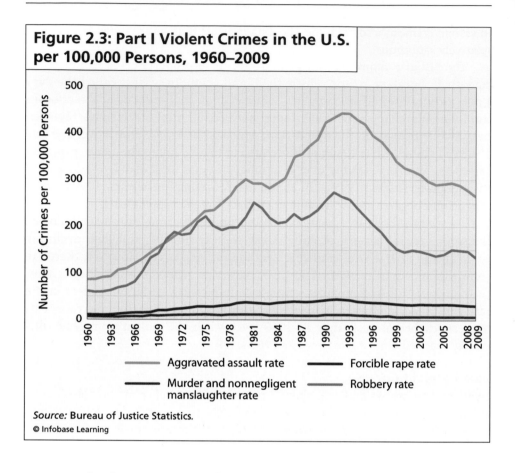

Figure 2.3: Part I Violent Crimes in the U.S. per 100,000 Persons, 1960–2009

Aggravated assault rate   Forcible rape rate

Murder and nonnegligent manslaughter rate   Robbery rate

Source: Bureau of Justice Statistics.
© Infobase Learning

extreme of violent crimes, murders are relatively rare. But given the brutality of this crime, murders are almost always reported to the police, a detail that makes murder-related data highly valid. About 90 percent of those arrested on murder charges are males; most women arrested for murder are charged with killing their husbands. The rate of offense is highest among those aged 18 to 24, and victims are most likely to be from the same age group. Far from being random, murders most commonly occur within social relationships, including spousal relations (and love triangles); among acquaintances; or at workplaces or schools. Homicide by strangers continues to be rare, but rates for this crime are rising.

One group that intrigues people is serial killers, who are defined as those who kill three or more victims in three or more separate incidents. Serial killers may act out of a variety of motivations. The generic "serial killer" classification includes goal-oriented expedience killers who typically kill for profit; mission killers who believe they are fulfilling a special vision to change the world; or thrill killers who kill while pursuing sexual pleasure or dominance. Mass murderers, those who kill four or more people in a single event, also garner great public attention. Many of the best known mass murders have undertaken attacks in public places, such as shopping areas, workplaces, or schools. They primary motives include vengeance, a twisted sense of loyalty to a person or cause, personal profit/advancement, or terrorism.

Rape

Forcible rape is commonly defined as an act where a man inflicts nonconsensual sexual intercourse upon a woman. Although there are other forms of sexual assault (male on male, female on female, or female on male), these acts do not fall within the traditional concept of rape. As with other forms of violent crime, the rape rate peaked in the early 1990s (at 42.8 per 100,000 in 1992) and since then declined markedly in the following decade (at 28.7 per 100,000 in 2009). These data must be interpreted carefully, for three reasons. First, crime statistics are reported as occurrences per 100,000 in the general population, but because rape victims arc most commonly female, we must consider the rate of rape per female in the population to be as much as 100 percent higher than for men. Second, a large number of rapes go unreported. In fact, NCVS data suggest that as many as 50 percent of rapes go unreported because victims are humiliated or believe that nothing will be done about the crime. Finally, there is a difference in how rape is defined: UCR data uses a narrow definition of rape, which includes only male-on-female incidents; the NCVS definition includes all forms of sexual assault.

Rape may be triggered by a number of factors (or combination of factors), including the culture of masculinity that stresses male dominance, psychological abnormalities, exposure to sexually oriented violence (including media

Anomalies in Rape Rates

For most crimes measured in UCR data and NCVS data, the trends in the two data sets match one another. One notable exception has been in rape rates. During some years in the late 1990s and early 2000s, the rape rate identified in UCR data seemed to stabilize, or even increase slightly; in contrast, NCVS data suggested that rape was on the decline. Criminologists argued that this discrepancy occurred as police agencies began to handle rape cases differently. During the 1980s and 1990s, more and more police agencies began creating special rape units that were taught to treat rape victims with more dignity and sensitivity than before. Thus, the consistency in the number of rape cases reported and recorded through UCR in the late 1990s and early 2000s very likely indicates that women were more willing to report rapes to the police.

portrayals), or the need to control others. According to research in sex offender characteristics, every rape includes at least one of the following: power, anger, or sadism. About 25 percent of rapes are gang rapes, those involving multiple offenders. A small proportion of rapists are serial offenders, who commit a series of rapes over time. However, the most common types of rape are **acquaintance rape** (involving someone known to the victim) and **date rape** (involving people in a dating relationship). **Statutory rape** involves an adult having sex with someone below the legal age of consent. Although the legal age of consent varies by state, the law typically stipulates that those who are below 14 or 16 years of age cannot legally consent to sexual relations. One view on rape that may surprise readers of this text is that in a longstanding traditional legal sense, a man could not be found guilty of raping his wife. This marital exemption is no longer valid under the law or in the eyes of most people in our society.

Aggravated Assault

The FBI defines **aggravated assault** as "an unlawful attack by one person upon another for the purpose of inflicting severe or aggravated bodily harm." Often assault and battery are conflated, as people might consider them part of the same act. The distinction is that battery requires actually touching another person, whereas assault involves attempting to harm another person or intentionally putting that person in a state of fear by word or deed. Battery commonly involves the use of blunt weapons (e.g., clubs) or hands and feet in an attack; threatening to use a blunt weapon or hands or feet (even if the victim is never actually touched) is assault.

Although assaults occur much more frequently than murders, the patterns observed in UCR data concerning assault are similar to those observed for murder. Namely, the rate of aggravated assault peaked in the early 1990s (at 441.9 per 100,000 in 1992) and subsequently declined to its present rate (at 262.8 per 100,000 in 2009). Similarly, about 80 percent of those identified as perpetrators and victims of assault are young men between the age of 18 and 24. Assault rates are highest in summer months, in urban areas, and in the Western and Southern regions of the country. A large subset of assaults occur between family members who perpetrate child abuse, sexual abuse, spousal abuse, or elder abuse. Assaults within this category are the focus of Chapter 4 of this book.

Robbery

Robbery is defined by the FBI as "the taking or attempting to take anything of value from the care, custody, or control of a person or persons by force or threat of force or violence and/or by putting the victim in fear." Robbery is a violent offense, not a property crime, because it involves force or intimidation to acquire money or property. Thus, it is a crime against a person or persons, rather than a property crime. In the early 1960s, the rate of robbery began to rise, though from 1974 until 1990 the rate of robbery hovered in the neighbor-hood of 200 to 250 per 100,000. After peaking in 1991 (at 272.7 per 100,000), the rate of robbery consistently declined over the following decade (at 133.0 per 100,000 in 2009). Thus, the pattern for robbery rates observed over the last half century has been somewhat different than for the other violent index crime. Specifically, the rate of robbery did not increase as much during the late 1970s and 1980s, although it did decline in a pattern consistent with the other violent Part I crimes.

Numerous types of robberies have been identified by criminologists. Rob-beries can occur in open areas, and these include street muggings and purse snatchings. In urban areas, this type of robbery comprises approximately 60 percent of all robberies reported. In addition, commercial establishments are often targeted in robberies, including banks, liquor stores, convenience stores, and restaurants. About 10 percent of robberies reported to police occur at pri-vate homes. Those committing robberies also fall into a variety of types, includ-ing professionals who pursue a career in robbery, those who happen upon opportunities to commit robbery, addicts who need to obtain money for drugs, and those who are under the influence of alcohol.

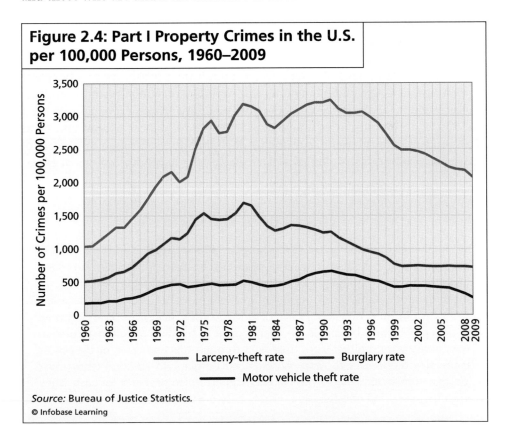

Figure 2.4: Part I Property Crimes in the U.S. per 100,000 Persons, 1960–2009

Larceny-theft rate   Burglary rate

Motor vehicle theft rate

Source: Bureau of Justice Statistics.

© Infobase Learning

Part I Property Crimes

Four crimes make up the FBI's list of Part I property crimes: burglary, larceny/ theft, motor vehicle theft, and arson. In all, property crimes make up about 92 percent of the total crime problem in any given year, and larceny is by far the most common of property crimes reported to police. Because arson statistics are often unreliable, most statistics about property crimes include only burglary, larceny, and motor vehicle theft. The general trends in these three crime categories constitute the property crime index as a whole, as illustrated in Figure 2.2. Here, Figure 2.4 illustrates the trends with respect to the Part I property crimes of burglary, larceny, and motor vehicle theft. Unlike violent crimes, which seem to have a wide variety of contributing causes, property crimes can be seen as arising from a narrower set of factors: psychological abnormality, substance abuse, the socialization process, and cultural values.

Burglary

Burglary is defined by the FBI as the unlawful entering of a residence, place of business, or other building with the purpose of committing another felony, characteristically theft. Burglary is often considered an inchoate crime, which means that it is a crime that is committed in the process of preparing for or committing another crime. Although many burglaries do include forced entry, unauthorized entry alone is sufficient to constitute burglary. According to the Bureau of Justice Statistics, it is estimated that about 70 percent of U.S. households will be burglarized at least once, although the probability of a burglary happening to a household in any one-year period is certainly much lower. Burglaries account for nearly 25 percent of all property crimes reported to police, and 70 percent of burglaries take place in private residences. About one-third of all residential burglaries occur during daylight hours, although 45 percent of nonresidential burglaries also take place during the day. Criminological expla-

Professional Burglars

Although most burglaries are opportunistic crimes perpetrated by offenders employing crude methods and little planning, a subset of burglars is professional and employs highly sophisticated methods. Career burglars may run highly profitable operations, may stay in the criminal enterprise for decades, and if caught, may be adept at avoiding long prison sentences. Learning how to be a professional burglar is strangely similar to learning a legitimate profession. Burglars must either learn their skills through trial and error, or they must apprentice themselves to more experienced burglars. In addition, they must locate and maintain reliable ways of exchanging stolen property for cash. They must therefore find or establish a reliable network within the illicit market.

nations for burglary involve the identification of places and times at which the following factors converge: the presence of a motivated offender (a burglar who wants something), the presence of a suitable target (a house or business where goods are stored), and the absence of guardians (such as a house where nobody is home and which does not have a burglar alarm or watchdog). Burglars range in their level of sophistication from those who are opportunistic, often youth who take advantage of unguarded homes, to those whose modus operandi are highly advanced and involved in professional burglar rings.

Larceny/theft

Larceny/theft is defined by the FBI as the unlawful removal of property from the effective possession of another person or its rightful location. Nearly two-thirds of all property crimes are thefts, making theft the most commonplace of all serious crimes. Theft may occur in combination with burglary, although only about 11 percent of theft occurs in buildings. About one-third of all thefts

Credit Card Theft/Fraud

The misuse of credit cards in the United States has been responsible for over $1 billion in annual losses for credit card issuers. The patterns are similar to burglary, with the vast majority of credit card misuse occurring after cards have been stolen during the commission of a robbery or a theft and are then used by the perpetrators of these crimes (or other criminals) at retail establishments. There

are, however, a small number of thieves who engage in credit card misuse in a professionally sophisticated way. For example, credit card rings may exploit databases to gather credit card numbers and personal information about a large number of credit card holders. This information may then be used to divert merchandise to false or fabricated addresses, where they may be collected by members of the credit card ring. Credit card theft and fraud is seen as a rising form of theft; fortunately for account holders, federal law limits consumer liability to $50 per credit card.

Collection of credit cards. As electronic commerce becomes the norm, criminal efforts to exploit credit card systems has flourished. (Shutterstock)

occur when property is removed from motor vehicles, and an additional 15 percent of thefts involve shoplifting from retail establishments. Perhaps surprisingly, other well-known forms of theft are relatively rare; for example, pick pocketing and purse snatching together account for less than 1 percent of thefts. Larceny does not involve the use of force or unlawful entry, and therefore does not generate as high a level of public fear as do related crimes such as robbery (a crime against a person which involves theft) and burglary (which involves entering a structure). Most larceny involves objects of low value, and therefore criminologists frequently distinguish between **petty larceny** (also known as petit larceny) of objects valued less than $50 or $100, and **grand larceny**, which involves goods of greater value. Petty larceny is punishable by fines or brief jail time, while grand larceny may be punished by prison sentences of as long as 20 years in some cases.

Motor Vehicle Theft

A particular type of larceny that is separately monitored by the FBI is **motor vehicle theft** (also known as grand theft auto), which is defined as the unlawful stealing or attempt to steal any motor vehicle, including an automobile, truck, motorcycle, or any other motorized vehicle. Motor vehicle thefts occur for many reasons, ranging from a short-term joyride to long-term transportation, from gaining prestige or enjoyment to making a profit, or even as a crime committed in the process of committing another crime. While it is true that some luxury

Motor vehicle with broken windows after a theft. *(Wikipedia) (Wikipedia)*

Grand Theft Auto

Motor vehicle theft is also known as grand theft auto in many jurisdictions. But in recent years, when folks use the term "Grand Theft Auto" (or GTA), they have been referring to a series of video games in which the player navigates the criminal underworld of a fictional city. GTA is often understood as a satire of the criminogenic environment observed in many American cities, but the game has generated quite a bit of controversy. Because the player assumes the role of criminal and because the criminal is the hero in the game, some critics find the entire game problematic. Other critics focus on specific activities that are role-played during GTA. For example, characters in the game might engage in sexual relations with prostitutes or drive drunk. Due to its controversial nature and content, GTA has been blamed as the inspiration or motivation for a number of real-life crimes, and the producers and distributors of the game have been subject to law suits.

cars are stolen at proportionately high rates, the bulk of cars stolen are rather nondescript. Cars and pickups that are commonly seen and which have been in production for a number of years are frequently targeted by car theft rings that run **chop shops** where stolen vehicles are stripped of their parts, which are then illegally sold. When cars are stolen while the owner is driving the vehicle, the crime is known as a **carjacking**. Though the event does include a motor vehicle theft, it is primarily considered a robbery, because it involves violence or threat of violence against a person. Motor vehicle theft has typically been combated via two methods: by making it more difficult to steal vehicles by installing alarms or kill switches, or by using tracking systems to help locate vehicles once they've been stolen.

Arson

The final variety of serious property crime tracked by the FBI is arson, defined as the intentional and unlawful burning of a vehicle, building (such as a home or place of business), or wild lands. Arson is responsible for the destruction of property and can also be the cause of injuries to persons. Although the FBI does track data for arson, these data are often omitted from criminology textbooks. Because it is often difficult to establish whether or not a fire was intentional, the data are considered unreliable. Many fires are set by juveniles, almost exclusively young and adolescent boys, whose motives may be relatively innocuous (such as accidental fires set off while playing) or may be cries for help. At the other end of the spectrum are more malicious motives, including the willful destruction of property and fire setting as an expression of serious psychological disturbances. Adults who set fires often do so for financial gain, sometimes with the intent of taking advantage of insurance claims on destroyed building and merchandise, or to eliminate obsolete vehicles or machinery or business competition. Another category of adult fire setters is motivated by emotional satisfaction derived from starting fires, a condition that might be indicative of psychological abnormalities. Given that some arsonists, both juvenile and adult, may be motivated to set fires because of mental illnesses, some critics contend that arson should not be considered criminal but should be viewed as symptomatic of mental illness.

SUMMARY

Establishing typologies for crime, the collection and maintenance of accurate crime data, and the monitoring of these data to identify trends are among the key concerns of the criminological enterprise. Some of the data collected are more valid than others, although all have some inherent and systematic flaws. Still, the UCR and the NCVS data are among the best available, and they do tell us a lot about the extent of the crime problem as well as about the trends associated with the problem. Some statistics are probably more valid than others. For example, nearly all murders are recognized as such, and therefore are likely reported to the police. This means that the numbers recorded in UCR data are likely to match closely the true extent of this crime. On the other hand, less severe crimes may be greatly underreported, either because victims don't notice, don't care, or don't believe any good will come of reporting the crime. Crime is unique as a subset of deviance because it is tracked and studied in national-level databases. No similar tracking of rates and trends exists for deviance that constitutes violations of folkways and mores.

Further Reading

Bureau of Justice Statistics. Publications. Available at http://bjs.ojp.usdoj.gov/.

Conklin, John. *Why Crime Rates Fell.* New York: Allyn and Bacon, 2003.

Cromwell, Paul (ed.). *In Their Own Words: Criminals on Crime,* 5th ed. New York: Oxford University Press, 2009.

Federal Bureau of Investigation. Crime in the U.S. Available at http://www.fbi.gov/about-us/cjis/ucr/crime-in-the-u.s/.

Federal Bureau of Investigation. Uniform crime reports. Available at http://www.fbi.gov/about-us/cjis/ucr/ucr.

Wilson, Colin. *A Criminal History of Mankind.* London, UK: Mercury Books, 2005.

Wright, R., and Decker, S. *Burglars on the Job: Streetlife and Residential Break-ins.* Boston: Northeastern University Press, 1994.

Zimring, Franklin. *The Great American Crime Decline.* New York: Oxford University Press, 2006.

CHAPTER 3

SOCIOLOGICAL PERSPECTIVES ON DEVIANCE AND CRIME

Because human behaviors are varied and complex, sociologists utilize theoretical perspectives to help understand often confusing behaviors such as deviance and crime. In general, we can identify four major sociological viewpoints on crime and deviance: objectivist thinking, subjectivist thinking, harm-based thinking, and the conflict perspective. Although no single perspective is capable of explaining all forms of deviance, each perspective has its strong points and is useful for explaining some forms of deviant behavior.

The first way of interpreting behaviors is via **objectivist** thinking, which involves the assumption that behaviors are either normative or deviant in themselves. The objectivist perspective assumes that actions have an independent essence that exists separate from the person committing the act, the person affected by the act, and the person who interprets or judges the act. Thus, from the objectivist perspective certain acts are simply wrong in themselves, as in the case when laws prohibit actions that are *mala in se.* Thus, the rightness or wrongness of an action does not lie within the details of the action, but rather emerges from the social sense of whether the act is appropriate, and this sensibility is independent of the act itself. The logic of objectivist thinking is also present in sociological approaches that view social reality as objective facts, separate from those observing its existence. For example, many people believe that killing another person is inherently wrong, and that regardless of context, the taking of another human life is never justified.

The second way of interpreting behaviors is via **subjectivist** thinking, which involves examining behaviors, not as inherently deviant, but rather defined as deviant because of the context in which they occur or how they are interpreted. The subjectivist approach assumes that actions have little or no objective essence, and that the rightness or wrongness of the act lies in the details concerning the person committing the act, the person affected by the act, and the person who interprets or judges the act. From the purely subjectivist perspective nothing is inherently wrong in itself unless defined as such, as in the case of laws that are *mala prohibitium*. Thus, the (in)appropriateness of a behavior lies within the details of the actions and how they are interpreted. All judgments about the deviancy of a behavior must therefore take into consideration where, when, how, and why an act occurs.

THEORETICAL PERSPECTIVES

One school of thought associated with objectivist thinking about deviance is known as **structural functionalism**, which views society as analogous to a biological system in which interdependent institutions fulfill complementary roles that comprise a coherent system. A functionalist thinker might point out that deviance has existed in every known society, and therefore that it must fulfill some important purpose. Just as exposure to pathogens stimulates the immune response in the body, a functionalist would argue that deviance provides an analogous system-strengthening function for society. Therefore, in this perspective the simple fact that deviance exists in all societies is evidence that deviance fulfills a positive function in any social system, because it helps to stimulate social solidarity among group members and helps to define the social boundaries of the group. For example, a horrific crime such as a terrorist attack serves to unite the group affected by the attack, as the members of the group temporarily put aside their differences to unite in solidarity against the terrorists and their messages. A more common example (for better or worse) is cliques formed by young people who share similar views on what is "normal" and unite in solidarity against someone who is "deviant" by virtue of not fitting the desired image or behavior.

A school associated with subjectivist thinking about deviance is the **social constructionist** approach, which views the normative sense of society as emerging out of efforts to define and interpret behaviors. As part of social life, individuals, groups, and institutions are constantly engaged in the process of defining social behavior and social life, and the rightness or wrongness of a behavior can be explained as the sum total of human efforts to define and interpret that behavior. Simply put, the social constructionist argues that something is appropriate if a social group deems it acceptable; along the same lines, something is prohibited if the social group agrees that it is unacceptable. The strength of the social constructionist approach is that it adequately explains how legal and

From a structural functionalist perspective, deviance can help to stimulate social solidarity and to define the social boundaries of a group. *(Shutterstock)*

moral standards change over time. For example, during the Prohibition Period of 1920 to 1933 in the United States, production and consumption of alcohol were strictly outlawed. Prohibition was repealed in 1933, and legal production and consumption of alcohol resumed. A constructionist would argue that the social standards concerning alcohol changed as society's attitudes toward the behavior changed over time.

As the text above and the examples illustrating objectivist and subjectivist approaches show, these approaches are diametrically opposed to one another. Two alternative conceptual approaches to studying and interpreting deviance have emerged: the harm-based approach and the conflict approach. The **harm-based approach** fits a middle ground between objectivity and subjectivity, in that it required both objective verification of harm as well as the subjective sense that harm is being incurred by some persons, group, or society. On the other hand, the **conflict approach** points to the disproportionate ability of some groups to define the social norms and to make their subjective interests appear to be the objective consensus of the society as a whole.

In the harm-based approach to deviance, both the objective and subjective elements must be satisfied, otherwise a behavior cannot be considered deviant.

New York City Deputy Police Commissioner John A. Leach watches agents pour liquor into a sewer during Prohibition. *(Library of Congress)*

For example, domestic violence, while it may often have been considered normal in past centuries, is now considered deviant within the harm-based approach because it causes objective physical and psychological harm to its victims and to family units, and at the same time it is generally recognized as ethically and morally inappropriate social behavior.

As noted above, the social conflict approach to deviance views the standards for behavior as primarily defined by powerful groups to protect their own interests. Powerful groups, by virtue of their privileged position in society, exert disproportionately more influence over processes of defining and enforcing standards for social behaviors. These groups may derive power from wealth, gender, race, religion, national origin, or other forms of social prestige. Within the social conflict approach, one can interpret many laws as supporting the interests of the rich, such as the way in which laws relating to commercial interests protect the interests of those who actually have commercial interests. This approach can also be applied to standards for behavior imposed on women (e.g., young women who engage in sex with numerous partners may be viewed with disdain, while young men exhibiting the same behavior may be viewed in a positive light) and may serve to control women's behavior in general while it benefits men who as a class occupy a relatively more powerful social position. In addition, the enforcement of rules might be skewed in favor of those in more powerful positions, as when illegal drug use among impoverished persons is more strongly patrolled and punished than illegal drug use among the middle or elite classes. An advantage of the conflict approach is that it is capable of explaining cases in which the definition or application of rules concerning social behaviors is inequitable or biased. However, one weakness of the conflict approach is that those with disproportionately higher power to define norms, and therefore who are more likely to benefit from those definitions, may often be unaware that they occupy a privileged position.

Taken together, the objectivist, subjectivist, harm-based, and conflict approaches to understanding deviance and crime are an intellectual tool-kit for understanding the oftentimes puzzling behaviors that transgress social norms. The traditional view of theft in the West African Ibo culture serves as an illustrative example. Ibos felt that someone stealing another's property would not be considered guilty of the crime if the owner failed to recognize that the theft had taken place. Thus, if someone stole some eggs from another person's chicken coop, it would not be a crime unless the owner noticed that the eggs were gone. In the case where the owner had numerous chickens, and presumably numerous eggs, it was unlikely that a small number of missing eggs would make a difference to the owner. On the other hand, if the owner had only one or two chickens, then he would immediately recognize that his expected eggs were missing, and therefore he would recognize the crime.

A number of aspects of this case help us to understand the complexity of perspectives on deviant behaviors. While traditional Ibo culture prohibited theft as an *objective* behavior, the fact that the owner must recognize that his property is missing added a *subjective* element to the cultural understanding of the crime. We can clearly see that the *harm-based approach* is reflected in the traditional Ibo cultural wisdom, in that for a theft of eggs to take place, there must be two conditions: verification that someone has stolen some eggs and the owner's recognition that the eggs have been stolen. On the other hand, the Ibo understanding of theft also reflects a *social conflict* sort of approach, though one that is aligned with the interests of the subordinate group. Traditional Ibo culture valued material success but condemned extravagance. Those who amassed a great deal of property would have difficulty monitoring it, and therefore the wealthy would be more vulnerable to pilfering than the poor. Because most of the population was less affluent than the few who had amassed wealth, the Ibo norms about theft served to distribute some wealth to the less affluent members of society.

Objectivity, Subjectivity, and in Between

Given the variety of human behaviors, and the variety of contexts in which they can take place, it is necessary for sociologists to employ a variety of approaches to understanding deviant and criminal behaviors. After all, behavior that might be entirely appropriate in one context might be entirely inappropriate in another. Certainly, there are some acts that appear to be *mala in se*, such as murder and rape, however even in the extreme case of homicide, many killings are considered acceptable. For example, police may use deadly force in apprehending or defending themselves against suspected criminals, and many states practice capital punishment. Thus, even acts that are almost universally prohibited may at times be appropriate under certain circumstances. This of course, leads logically to the idea that acts may be deviant only when they are defined as such.

On the other hand, many folks are dissatisfied with the idea that morals are inherently relative and would argue that a purely subjective approach to deviance does not serve the interests of the wider society. Thus, social scientists struggle to find a reasonable perspective that helps clarify the objective nature of social consensus about morality and the subjective tendency for social standards to change over time or within different contexts.

This said, the utility of varying perspectives on deviance and crime is that they help us to understand social behaviors from diverse points of view. This moves us forward to a more intentional and comprehensive view of social behaviors, and helps us understand deviance not only from our own subjective

The Saints and the Roughnecks

In 1973, sociologist William J. Chambliss published what has become a seminal piece in the sociology of deviance and in juvenile delinquency studies. Chambliss described an American town in which there were two cliques of adolescent males: "the saints" who were from middle-class families and "the roughnecks" who were from working-class families. Chambliss observed that the members of both groups tried to duck out of school early; on weekends they engaged in a variety of petty offenses, including drinking, fighting, and being a nuisance. While both groups exhibited similar behaviors, the saints' school grades were markedly better than those of the roughnecks, and the saints were treated much better by authority figures (including police). Chambliss suggests that the town in general was biased toward the saints and tended to be much more forgiving of their misbehavior than of similar behaviors exhibited by the roughnecks. Chambliss also noted that, years after the initial observance, the saints as a whole had achieved much higher career success than the roughnecks. It seems that the bias favoring the saints had helped them to achieve much greater levels of success in life, whereas the roughnecks' life chances were more limited.

points of view, but also as social phenomena reflective of diverse and complex societies.

EXAMINING THE CAUSES OF CRIME AND DEVIANCE

In the previous section, we explored the conceptual ways of studying crime and deviance. The focus of this section is the examination of the motivations and causes behind deviant behaviors. One way of examining the motivations is to distinguish between instrumental and expressive acts. **Instrumental acts** are those designed to achieve some sort of goal, whether overt or implied. Examples of this might be the professional burglar who chooses burglary as a career (or a way to make a living) or the addict who mugs people on the street to get money to feed the addiction. Because 92 percent of crimes are related to property, it is clear that much of criminal behavior has instrumental motivations.

Another variety of deviant and criminal behaviors are **expressive acts**, which are those behaviors intended to communicate some sort of message, whether overt or implied. Examples are the graffiti artist who paints a symbol on a building in an effort to communicate that the location is considered the territory of a particular gang or terrorists who attack innocent civilians in an attempt to convey their political message.

Of course, the expressiveness or instrumentality of an act lies on a continuum, and most deviant acts are in fact some combination of the two. The following examples of crimes and deviant behaviors reflect this confluence of instrumental and expressive and also reflect that the balance between expressive and instrumental is fluid. Some perpetrators of violent crimes want to gain power or control over others (instrumental), a desire related to many rapes or murders in which offenders exert physical or psychological control over their victims (expressive). Other offenders may engage in deviance for the sake of generating excitement or relieving boredom (instrumental). Young people may steal a car for a joyride, or they may use prohibited substances to enjoy the high they get, not only from the substance, but also from the process of overcoming risks associated with the behavior (expressive). Other deviant or criminal acts may take place as part of the process of identity-seeking (instrumental). Oppositional youth subcultures (e.g., street gangs or skinheads), as well as many of the deviant behaviors and attitudes associate with them, may be interpreted as the expression of the members' efforts to seek a functioning identity and define their personal and group relationship with the mainstream society. Finally, some actions are almost purely expressive, and the acts themselves are the means of conveying a message, as in the case of terrorists or mass murders who perpetrate horrible violence as a way of expressing their dissatisfaction with some aspects of social life.

Although instrumentality and expressiveness are important elements to examine when trying to understand the motivations behind crimes and deviance,

Mental Illness as a Cause of Crime

Many persons convicted of serious crimes exhibit some degree of mental disorder, including depression, personality disorders, or substance abuse issues. Despite these disorders, these individuals are held responsible for their actions. Only those who suffer from psychosis (a condition characterized by a loss of contact with reality) are relieved of their responsibility. Because they do not understand what is real, people with psychosis cannot have malicious intent, and therefore, pursuant to the legal definition of such criminal acts, cannot be considered criminals. Those who suffer from other mental disorders and do understand the fundamental nature of reality are held accountable for their actions. Sociologically, we can thus understand mental disorders as contributing to the crime problem while also understanding that those who suffer from psychosis are not criminal because they cannot demonstrate *mens rea*.

they don't necessarily get to the heart of what might cause or drive such behaviors in the first place. What is more germane is the role of choice and the role of external factors that might influence or provoke criminal or deviant acts. These factors are explored in the following section.

Theories of Crime Causation

There are two basic varieties of criminological theories. **Choice theories** point to the role that independent human decision making plays in determining social behaviors. The idea that individuals choose the paths of their behavior is certainly not new; it has been a facet of both scientific and common sense thinking about social action since the Age of Enlightenment in the late 18th century. Prior to the Enlightenment, Western tradition and jurisprudence held that those committing criminal or deviant acts were possessed by evil spirits. The Enlightenment's introduction of the concept that personal choice played a crucial role in causing social behaviors was, at the time, a radically new idea, one that forms the basis of what is known as classical criminology. The assumption was that individuals were rational and endowed with the ability to determine their own actions.

To choose among the variety of possible actions available, individuals were assumed to engage in a cost-benefits analysis in which they attempted to maximize their pleasure and/or to minimize their pain. This rational calculus drove individual decision making concerning whether to engage in normative or deviant behavior. The process underlying the theory works as follows.

Presumably, when engaging in criminal or deviant behaviors, individuals may be subject to negative social sanctions, such as punishments or social criticisms. It follows that the person contemplating a criminal or deviant act would perceive that there are potential liabilities to engaging in behavior that transgressed the norm. That same individual, however, would recognize that there might also be benefits to violating norms, profits from a crime, for example. Seeing the potential benefits and pitfalls, the individual would then engage in the process of weighing the advantages versus the disadvantages for each action. It was presumed that the rational actor would always choose to maximize pleasure, or at least to minimize pain. This logic is intimately tied to the development of the concept of **deterrence**, which is the concept that individuals may be discouraged from engaging in norm violating behavior, when the penalties for those violations are severe. Though the idea of choice was important in the foundation of crime and deviancy studies, it fell out of favor for many years as social science more deeply explored the social structural aspects of crime causation.

Execution of conspirators involved in the assassination of Abraham Lincoln. Some argue that harsh punishments act as a deterrent to crime. *(Wikipedia)*

As choice theory became less popular, other social thinkers increasingly pointed to factors outside the individual, which might be important in determining (or at least influencing) behaviors. These **structural theories**, as they were called, pointed to factors beyond the control of the individual, which determined social behaviors. Included in this category were some early theories regarding the role that factors such as body type and the shape of a person's head might play in disposing certain types toward criminality, but these factors have now been entirely discredited. The structural factors that continue to be relevant in studying crime and deviancy are social structural factors, such as aspects of social inequality (such as poverty). The earliest social structural thinkers tended to conduct localized studies of the social environment of cities, or even neighborhoods within cities. For example, early criminologists noted that a large proportion of crimes occurring within a city seemed to take place within a small number of neighborhoods within the city. By studying these neighborhoods, they discerned that neighborhoods with high incidence of crime often had high rates of poverty, low stability of residence, and deteriorating or weakened social institutions, such as schools, churches, and civic groups. Thus, the highly **criminogenic** aspect of such neighborhoods could be associated with aspects of the social institutions that operated within them. Through studying these neighborhoods over time, criminologists were able to establish that the members of any cultural group who occupied the distressed neighborhoods in question showed a high level of criminality, but that when they moved out of these neighborhoods, their proclivity for crime and deviancy declined.

In the contemporary world, the field of crime and deviancy studies tends to be dominated by sociologists and other social scientists who focus primarily on the social structural aspects that might influence the members of certain groups, or those living in certain contexts, disproportionately toward criminality and deviancy. Among the additional things examined as structural factors are aspects of the socialization of youth, the role that institutions of socialization (e.g., schools, family, and peer groups, which are all discussed in connection with juvenile delinquency in Chapter 7) play in crime and deviancy, and the influence that repressive social relations might have on the development of deviant lifestyles.

Social scientists have identified a variety of factors that are generally related to variations in crime rates. These include:

- *Climate, temperature, and region.* Crimes occur at higher rates in late summer months (e.g., July and August) and also vary according to temperature—low in cold temperatures, rising as weather warms to the mid-80s, and then declining as temperatures become extremely hot (above 85). The Northeast and Midwest regions of the country have lower rates than the West and the South.

- *Poverty.* Persons living in poverty exhibit a higher rate of criminal offense, and impoverished neighborhoods have higher crime rates (two factors which are related). While some argue that the poor may have an economic motivation to commit crimes (especially property crimes), most sociologists cite poverty as a factor that disrupts two crucial aspects of the social order: the ability of individuals to develop into well-adjusted members of society, and the ability of communities to protect themselves from motivated offenders.
- *Gender.* The rate of offense for most crimes is higher for males than for females. This difference is attributed to a number of factors. First, women and girls may be socialized to live in relationships with others, and therefore gender differences may be attributable to the socialization process. In contrast, men and boys are more commonly socialized to value aggression, toughness, and competition. In a cognitive sense, the differences may also be explained by the tendency for men to express frustration in outwardly aggressive ways, while women are more likely to internalize social difficulties and are more prone to anxieties and depression.
- *Race.* Statistics suggest that African Americans as a group have a higher level of criminal offense than whites, Native Americans have rates of offense similar to whites, and Asians have significantly lower rates of offense than whites. It is unlikely that the persistently high rate of offense observed in African Americans is caused by attributes of race or culture; most criminologists explain these differences in terms of bias in the justice system (which treats African American offenders more harshly) and economic disparity (as a disproportionately high number of African Americans live in poverty).
- *Age.* The influence of age on criminal offenses is so widely accepted that it is almost axiomatic. The tendency is for crime to vary according to the life cycle. Children, middle-aged people, and elderly people are almost never criminal offenders. The majority of criminal offenses are committed by adolescents and young adults. Specifically, the rate of violent offense increases in late adolescence, peaks at age 18, and then declines over the life course. Similarly, property offenses increase in late adolescence, peak at age 16, and then decline sharply. Most property offenses drop by half by age 20, and after age 20, the rate declines steadily over the life course.

Although structural theories may be helpful in explaining why certain groups may violate norms at higher rates, the structural approach is incapable of clarifying why two individuals within the same social context might make entirely different choices for their actions. Some violate the norms, and others conform. One explanation for this anomaly is the concept of rational choice.

In recent years, the concept of **rational choice** has received increased attention in academic studies of crime and deviance. In contemporary applications of this theory, one must examine the decision-making process of individuals within a framework that considers that rationality is likely to be situational. What this means is that a rational choice for one person in a given situation or context may not be the rational choice for another person in an entirely different context. The concept of rational choice gives credit to the offenders (who after all may be very motivated and creative) by conceptualizing them as reasoning beings who make intelligent choices based on information that is available to them. The rational choices made by these individuals can fall in two areas. The first is an offense rationality. Here an offender considers which sorts of crimes might best suit his or her skills and aptitudes. Thus, a potential offender might actually choose the type of crime to commit. The second sort of rationality comes when the offender approaches the specific crime and can work actively to select the specific target and context that appear most vulnerable (e.g., because the target is not protected, or because there is little chance of getting caught).

Contemporary social thinkers tend to view rational choice as being a relevant factor in determining the causality of crime and deviance, although social scientists also acknowledge the importance of understanding the context in which that decision occurs. For example, it is difficult to understand how individuals who are afforded every advantage in life (e.g., affluence, education, nice lifestyle), choose to commit crimes. On the other hand, it is also difficult to understand how persons who are presented in life with every imaginable obstacle (e.g., poverty, poor education, exposure to drugs and violence), choose to live well-adjusted lives as law-abiding citizens. From these two extremes, one can see the limitations of seeing social behavior as caused entirely by either structural factors or choice. By combining the two aspects (choice and structure), however, we can see that those who are presented with advantages in life are less likely to offend, whereas those who are presented with impediments and disadvantages are more likely to offend. Nonetheless, the relationship is not absolute because individuals exert their autonomy and do not always fall into expected or predicted behaviors. Thus, many social scientists occupy a middle ground between pure objectivity and pure subjectivity in understanding crime and deviance, and a similar middle ground exists with regards to the identification of the factors causing crime and deviance. In short, contemporary scholars of crime and deviance recognize the interplay of both structural factors and choice in determining social behavior and also recognize that theories are neither absolute nor infallible.

SUICIDE AND SELF–INJURY

Suicide has been among the most studied forms of deviant behavior, and although it might seem like an entirely personal choice, sociologists have identified many structural factors that promote such behavior. This provides an excellent opportunity to examine the interplay between individual choices and external factors that influence suicide and related behaviors. On the one hand, it is clear that suicide is a behavior that an individual might choose, but sociologists also observe that suicide rates vary according to key sociological factors. For example, a sociologist might examine factors that cause more members of one group to engage in suicide as well as factors that influence members of another group to eschew this behavior. Within this difference it is apparent that individuals are conscious of their choices, although external factors may push members of some groups toward suicide at a higher rate (while pulling members of other groups away from suicide, resulting in a lower rate for that group).

Suicide is literally the act of causing one's own death. Sociologically, **suicide** is defined as the intentional act of self-injury or potential self-injury where the person undertaking the action cannot be sure of survival. Thus, actual self-killing and attempted self-killing fall both fall under the definition of suicide. An interesting detail is that suicide can also be active or passive. It can result from

Suicide prevention message on the Golden Gate Bridge. Sociologists understand that suicide behaviors follow patterns, and study of these patterns can lead to interventions. *(Wikipedia. Photo by David Corby)*

active self-injury (as in the case of someone who does something purposely to end life) or from passive self-injury (as in the case of someone who does not take actions to preserve life, such as not moving out of the way of an on-coming vehicle).

The medical and psychiatric causes of suicide have been widely studied, although these lie outside of the scope of this sociological text. Suffice it to say that a variety of psychological causes have been associated with suicidal behaviors, including mental illnesses (e.g., depression and mood disorders), substance abuse issues (such as alcohol and drug dependencies), and problem gambling behaviors. Numerous fundamental sociological factors have also been identified as relating to suicide. For example, it is estimated by the World Health Organization that approximately 60 percent of suicides occurring worldwide take place in Asian countries, especially China, India, and Japan. In the United States, the white population has a suicide rate of approximately 2.5 times that of blacks and Hispanics. Clearly, there is a connection between self-killing and social attitudes about such behavior—in some cultural contexts suicide may be more acceptable (or at least less stigmatized) than in others.

In the United States, there are approximately 33,000 deaths by suicide per year, which amounts to an annual rate of approximately 11 per 100,000 in the population. The suicide rate for men in the United States is approximately 18 per 100,000, while the rate for women is approximately 4.5 per 100,000. This difference is explained by the tendency of men to use more extreme (and therefore more certain) means of ending their own lives, such as firearms or jumping off buildings. Women tend to choose less certain methods, such as overdosing on medications. Typical social factors that appear to trigger suicide in Western cultures are unemployment, debt, despair, and social isolation.

A Teen Suicide Pact

In her 1998 book *Teenage Wasteland,* sociologist Donna Gaines recounts the story of four suburban teenagers from northern New Jersey who killed themselves in a suicide pact in 1987. The youth were from a working-class neighborhood, and they often felt excluded in school and social settings. As an expression of their perceived hopelessness for their future prospects, the four teenagers killed themselves by running a car inside a closed garage. *Teenage Wasteland* is considered a classic in cultural studies of youth subcultures, and helps clarify the disaffection that many young people experience.

Suicide pacts involve two or more people agree to kill themselves at the same time. Mass suicides, such as the one in Jonesboro, Guyana, are excluded from this category. Mass suicides often follow religious or political motivations, whereas suicide pacts take place as a shared expression of personal despair.

Doctor-Assisted Suicide

Physician-assisted suicide refers to cases in which a medical practitioner helps patients, typically terminally ill patients, to end their lives. The doctor does not directly cause the death of the patient (which would be considered euthanasia, a practice that is widely banned), but typically provides the patient with lethal doses of a drug that can be self-administered. The most famous case of physician-assisted suicide involved Dr. Jack Kevorkian (colloquially known as "Dr. Death") who created a device that would allow patients to administer a lethal dose of a drug intravenously. Dr. Kevorkian is an iconic figure in what is known as the "Right to Die" movement, sometimes also called the "Death with Dignity" movement. In 1999, Kevorkian was convicted of murder when he helped a terminally ill ALS patient to end his own life. He served 8 years in prison and was released in 2007, under the condition that he would not practice medicine or counsel anyone regarding methods to end life. Currently, physician-assisted suicide is legal in three states (Montana, Oregon, and Washington), in many European countries (e.g., France, Germany, and Switzerland), and in Japan.

In most contexts, suicidal behaviors (even suicidal thoughts) are by definition interpreted as being indicative of mental illness. Thus, persons who are feeling suicidal are often provided with interventions designed to prevent them from attempting to injure themselves. In the United States, persons contemplating suicide are often considered legally incompetent to refuse medical treatment and can therefore be transported by law enforcement or paramedics directly to a hospital emergency room, where they will receive psychological treatment for their condition. This is a frequently contested legal point, as some argue that those facing terminal illness should be allowed to end their own lives.

Generally, social norms prohibit suicidal behaviors, and many states and countries have laws that prohibit suicide. Ironically, these laws are ineffectual against those who commit suicide because it is impossible to punish the actual perpetrators. In a practical sense, however, most anti-suicide laws target individuals who are present at a suicide or aid and abet a suicide. Many moral codes, especially those based on religious principles, strictly prohibit suicide. For example, in the Judeo-Christian and Muslim religious traditions, the prohibition against self-killing derives from the general prohibition against killing. On the other hand, there are instances that suicide is not only condoned but socially approved. People who risk their own lives to save the lives of others are hailed as heroes; people willing to die rather than renounce a religious belief or a moral principle are deemed martyrs. For example, police and firefighters who risk their own lives for the sake of others' safety are held in particularly high regard.

Suicide Attacks

Throughout history, there have been various examples of suicide attacks. Perhaps the most famous were the Japanese *kamikaze* of World War II, pilots who deliberately crashed explosive-laden planes into military targets. The term *kamikaze* translates as "divine wind," and it was believed that executing such an attack was extremely honorable and would transport the pilot directly to heaven. More recently, we have also observed suicide bombings carried out on behalf of terrorist groups. Suicide bombers have strapped explosives to their own bodies or have driven vehicles and flown airplanes into targeted buildings. Such attacks are generally motivated by religious fervor or extreme nationalism. Fortunately such events are rare. The salient point here is that suicide bombers are willing to sacrifice their own lives for what they perceive to be a greater social benefit.

Although sociologists have been studying suicidal behaviors for many years, they have only recently started to study nonlethal forms of **self-injury**, which are defined as any intentional self-inflicted harm that a person performs on his or her own body. While suicide is the extreme end of the continuum of self-injury, other forms of self-injury vary greatly from widely accepted practices (such as self-piercing of ears) to strongly condemned practices (such as self-mutilation, including self-castration, and self-amputation). In the middle of this continuum are practices accepted by certain subcultures, which can include ritualized piercing, ritualized scarification, or tattooing. Such examples of self-harm are accepted (or even promoted) within their respective subcultures, but are not generally condoned by society at large. Other forms of self-injury are carried out by individuals and therefore do not fit within the behaviors of a subculture. Such forms of self-harm include self-cutting and bloodletting, self-inflicted burns, self-tattooing or scarification. These behaviors are often carried out in private and in secret and are generally considered symptomatic of psychiatric distress and viewed as deviant behavior that is widely condemned.

Suicide: Personal Choice or Environmental Structural Factors?

At first glance suicide behaviors appear to be the result of individual choice to cause self-harm, best explained by understanding the individual motivations toward self-killing. However, sociologists have noted that the rate of suicide varies from group to group, and this suggests that there might be sociological variables that also promote or deter suicide. From this perspective, suicidal behaviors are deviant behaviors that require an understanding of the interplay between choice and structural factors.

We can, of course, understand that suicides vary in motivation. Some individuals may select self-killing as a way to reach a goal (instrumental motivation). Examples might include avoiding dealing with great debt or avoiding being a burden on others. Other suicides appear motivated by the desire to send a message (expressive motivation). Indeed, many interpret the act of suicide as a cry for help, thus highlighting the communicative aspect of suicide behaviors. This interpretation is supported by suicide notes or other efforts to communicate, which are often an aspect of suicide events. In the middle ground, we can also interpret many suicides as combining efforts: to achieve some explicit or implicit goal and to communicate a message.

In his classical work on suicide, sociologist Émile Durkheim defined suicide as "all cases of death resulting directly or indirectly from a positive or negative act of the victim himself, which he knows will produce this result." Durkheim's primary intent was to study suicide behaviors as objective facts (i.e., as social events that exist independently of those individuals engaging in the suicide behavior). Whereas Durkheim considered only suicide events in which the persons had in fact killed themselves, later sociologists began to consider events in which persons tried to kill themselves but failed.

Durkheim's Suicide

In 1897, French sociologist Émile Durkheim published his groundbreaking study on suicide. Titled *Suicide*, the work became a foundational text in the field of sociology. In the text, Durkheim argued that sociological factors were keys to explaining the different rates of suicide observed among varying groups, and in particular, that proper measures of both internal and external social control were keys to lowering suicide rates. Durkheim identified four types of suicide:

- *Egoistic suicide.* Likely to occur when individuals have not developed sufficient levels of internal social control. Without a sense of belonging, individuals may feel socially disconnected and find life meaningless.
- *Altruistic suicide.* Likely to occur when individuals have an overly developed sense of internal social control. When the ego is overwhelmed by the weight of social pressure, the individual is more likely to sacrifice their personal interests for those of the group.
- *Anomic suicide.* Likely to occur in periods of rapid social change, when social norms are in a state of flux. During such periods, individuals may be confused about the validity of old and evolving social norms.
- *Fatalistic suicide.* Likely to occur in periods where social norms are excessive and do not allow room for adequate individual expression. In such periods, the individual may feel that life is hopeless.

Most sociologists have concluded that it is important to understand both the personal motivations and the meaning attributed to suicide behaviors. We note, for example, that suicide does contain elements of personal choice—individuals must plan and execute the act of suicide and, at the same time, must provide meaningful interpretations and social definitions (if even to themselves) for the act. On the other hand, we note that suicide rates vary, depending on and influenced by key sociological factors that include race, age, religion, gender, ethnicity, nationality, and socioeconomic status. Durkheim, for example, concluded that Catholics as a whole had a lower rate of suicide than Protestants, because Catholics had a higher level of group solidarity.

Similarly, we note that some nations have relatively high suicide rates, including some Eastern European countries (such as Belarus, Lithuania, Russia, and Ukraine) and some East Asian countries (such as South Korea and Japan). In other parts of the world, including some Caribbean countries (such as Jamaica, Haiti, and the Dominican Republic) and many Middle Eastern countries (such as Jordan, Syria, and Egypt), suicide rates are extremely low, and at times almost nil. Clearly, some larger effects are at work here, and structural factors (including culture, economy, and nation) converge to explain differing rates of suicide on group levels. In addition, the suicide rate for men is higher than the suicide rate from women in almost every country. This gender dynamic can also be seen as a structural factor influencing individual decisions to commit suicide, further illustrating the interplay between choice and structural factors in cases of suicide.

Death Row Volunteering

In recent decades, there has been the tendency for some individuals wishing to end their lives to use state-sanctioned means to achieve this goal. For example, about 11 percent of those executed in the United States are known as "death row volunteers," a name given to individuals who have received death sentences and who have elected to stop their legal appeals process, thereby hastening their own executions. There have been a number of famous cases, some of which have become the subject of books and even motion pictures. Examples include the cases of Aileen Wournos (subject of the 2003 film *Monster*), Gary Gilmore (subject of the book and film *Executioner's Song*), and Oklahoma City Bomber Timothy McVeigh. While some interpret the actions of the condemned as positively aiding the state to carry out its mandate, critics claim that the inmates demonstrate mental illnesses and are therefore using the state as a means to commit suicide.

Where Can Someone Find Help If Feeling Suicidal?

Those having suicidal thoughts can often feel alone and scared; however, there are places to seek help. In the U.S., there is a toll free helpline which is available 24 hours a day: 1-800-273-TALK (8255); 1-888-628-9454 (Spanish); 1-800-799-4889 (TTY). Those in other countries can visit the following web site to find helplines and other resources locally: http://www.befrienders.org/. If you believe that you or someone you know is in immediate danger of hurting themselves seriously or attempting suicide, it may be a good idea to call 911 to get emergency responders to the scene. The following web sites also offer useful information for those experiencing suicidal thoughts, or to their friends and family: http://helpguide.org/topics/suicide_prevention.htm and http://www.suicidepreventionlifeline.org.

SUMMARY

Examining the underlying causes and motivations for social behavior (especially those that violate established norms) is central to the sociological enterprise. Sociologists employ a variety of theoretical perspectives to understand deviance and crime, ones which consider the influences of structural contexts as well as personal choice. Suicide and other forms of self-injury might appear counter to rational choice, but there is incontrovertible evidence that choice does factor in suicide and self-injuring behaviors because some individuals will choose suicide whereas others (even in the worst of circumstances) will not. Clearly, human behaviors are extremely complex, and each behavioral decision reflects a confluence of individual and structural factors.

Further Reading

American Foundation for Suicide Prevention. Understanding and preventing suicide through research, education, and advocacy. Available at http://www.afsp.org/.

Chambliss, William J. "The Saints and the Roughnecks." *Society* 11 (1973): 24–31.

Durkheim, Émile. *Suicide: A Study in Sociology.* New York: Free Press, 1997 [originally 1897].

Gaines, Donna. *Teenage Wasteland: Suburbia's Dead End Kids.* Chicago: University of Chicago Press, 1998.

Joiner, Thomas. *Why People Die by Suicide.* Cambridge, Mass.: Harvard University Press, 2007.

Mind. Understanding self-harm. Available at http://www.mind.org.uk/help/diagnoses_and_conditions/self-harm.

Steel, Eric (director). *The Bridge.* Koch Lorber Films, 2007. DVD 94 min.

CHAPTER 4

VICTIMS AND VICTIMIZATION

Among the significant subfields within crime and deviancy studies, the study of crime victims stands out for its development as an academic field often closely associated with activist work. For those interested in helping victims of crimes, this is an area of sociology that seeks to assist victims by preventing crime and reducing the negative impacts on victims when crimes do take place. **Victimology** involves one or more of the following: understanding the role that the victim plays in the criminal process, understanding types and trends of victimization, and understanding the importance of the victim in the process of law enforcement and justice. Victimology can also extend to the study of the interplay between victims and social institutions (e.g., the media or the criminal justice system) and to noncriminal human rights violations (e.g., violations of fetal rights, reproductive rights, or rights to fair trade).

From a sociological point of view, crime is not a random phenomenon, and therefore neither is victimization. One of the theories that best describes the process of victimization is the **routine activities theory**, which argues that crimes (and hence victimization) occur most commonly where three factors converge: the presence of motivated offenders, the presence of suitable targets, and the absence of adequate guardians. For example, if a mugger spots a lone person walking in a deserted parking garage, that person may be targeted for a robbery if the garage is poorly lit or not otherwise guarded (e.g., by patrol or surveillance camera). The most **criminogenic** environments are those where the three factors overlap, and persons at highest risk of crime victimization are those whose routine activities take them into the presence of motivated offenders and away from effective guardians. Prostitutes, for example, are victimized fairly commonly, because their routine activities typically keep them in areas away from police patrols and because they commonly carry cash.

What complicates the picture is that victims and offenders may, at different times, be the same individuals or members of the same groups. In other words, the members of groups who are the most common offenders are also most commonly victimized. Just as a small subset of the population is responsible for a disproportionately high proportion of criminal offense (particularly violent offenses), members of those same groups are also victimized at a disproportionately high level.

It is perhaps surprising that crime victims traditionally did not receive much attention. But this is a more or less natural result of the way the legal system in the United States is structured. In the legal sense, society as a whole (not an individual) is considered to be the victim when a criminal act is committed. Thus victims are not (at least in a purely legal sense) considered relevant in legal proceedings. Victims can hardly be expected to act objectively, and therefore the state acts as the aggrieved party to ensure due process of law and to avoid the use of legal punishment as retribution. Thus, an assault case might be labeled "The State of California v. Jones," which indicates that the individual Jones is accused of violating the interests of the people and State of California (i.e., the interests of the entire society) and not solely the interests of the assault victim.

But what about victims? Does the criminal justice system have any responsibility to the victims of crime, or are victims simply an incidental by-product of a crime? Such a question lies at the heart of contemporary victimology, especially when the effects of crime victimization can be significant and long lasting. Almost all victims experience some sort of emotional distress from their

Who Is a Victim?

The United States collects data about victims using the annual National Crime Victimization Survey (NCVS) of households. The data collected through this survey indicate that the most victimized group in the country comprises men in their prime (aged 24 to 34) and that these individuals are most frequently victimized by strangers. These data contradict some common stereotypes of victims being members of comparatively vulnerable groups, such as the elderly and women. Similarly, the statistics compiled by the NCVS seem to dispel the idea that people are more likely to be victimized by people they know. Trends indicate that most forms of victimization have decreased sharply since the early to mid-1990s, and that victimization is currently at its lowest point in four decades.

Hans von Hentig's *The Criminal and His Victim*

Von Hentig's 1948 book *The Criminal and His Victim* is a foundational work in victimology studies, because von Hentig was among the first scholars to document the role that victims might play in a criminal interaction. Before this study, and indeed even today, most criminology tended to be offender oriented and ignored the role of victims in criminal acts. Von Hentig proposed that some victims were active participants in such acts, a notion that was far removed from the traditional opinion that victims were always the passive recipients of victimization. His study focused on characteristics of victims that were likely to provoke attacks by offenders, thereby precipitating victimization. Von Hentig pointed out that jurisprudence tended to make a clear distinction between the individual causing suffering and the individual on the receiving end of that suffering. Countering this perspective, he posited that a number of victims consented, cooperated, or provoked their own suffering. Such individuals, according to von Hentig, were more prone to victimization than others who played no role in precipitating their own victimization. Though von Hentig's work is often discredited, it has the distinction of being one of the earliest systematic studies in victimology.

victimization, and for many victims, the psychological effects result in fear, anxiety, feelings of shame, or self-blame. A subset of victims develops posttraumatic stress disorder, and the emotional responses to crime may exacerbate preexisting mental health issues in victims. Vulnerable populations, particularly children and the elderly, may experience these effects most acutely. For many victims, the lasting effects of their victimization may include a lingering sense of vulnerability, a sense of meaningless in life, and diminished self-worth.

One of the earliest studies of crime victims was conducted by German criminologist Hans von Hentig, who was among the first scholars to consider the characteristics of persons who were most frequently victimized and to note the important role that crime victims might play in their own victimization.

According to recent studies on the subject, victimization is more about one's environment and habits than about any inherent qualities of the potential victim. Sociologically, we can view a crime as a social interaction between two or more persons, and as with any social exchange, all the participants potentially play a role in determining the resolution of a given interaction. Hans von Hentig (see sidebar) suggested that some crime victims might bring about their own victimization by antagonizing offenders or encouraging offenders to escalate the level of an assault or other abuse, a concept known as **victim precipitation**. An example illustrating this point is an altercation during which both participants verbally and/or physically taunt their opponents, which might lead to an

Argument between two individuals. Is the woman's response to verbal abuse likely to defuse the situation or to escalate the level of the altercation? *(Shutterstock)*

escalation of violence. In the end, a participant who escalates the level of animosity may end up seriously injured or killed as a result. Although no reasonable person would claim that the victim deserved serious injury or death, it is possible to see that the victim played a role in bringing about the victimization.

Advocating for Victims

In criminal cases with women victims, the idea of victim precipitation has often been used to mitigate the offender's responsibility for the act, an interpretation that falls well outside the academic utility of the theory. Unfortunately, the concept of victim precipitation (first presented by von Hentig in 1948) continues to have common sense currency, even though it was (and continues to be) strongly criticized in scholarly work. It is likely that the first vocal critics of this theory were feminist scholars and other advocates of women's rights who pointed out that women victims, particularly those victimized in strongly gendered crimes such as forcible rape and domestic violence, were frequently blamed for their own victimization. For example, the criminal defense in a rape case often cited a woman's provocative behavior or dress, her sexual history, and any past liaisons with the offender as evidence that the victim might have precipitated her own victimization. Similarly, in cases of spousal abuse, the defense often suggested that the abused woman had somehow misbehaved, which they then suggested could justify her husband's need to use physical discipline.

Some critics also argued that the criminal justice system seemed to be more concerned with the fair treatment of offenders and the preservation of their rights, while victims were often made to feel even further victimized as a result of interactions with the criminal justice system. Understandably, feminists objected to this treatment of victims, citing the insensitivity of the criminal justice system particularly in cases involving sex-related and domestic offenses. The victims' rights movement emerged from the controversy and outcry surrounding the poor treatment of victims. A movement that was essentially created to improve the treatment of crime victims, it was also an extension of more broadly conceived efforts to ensure human rights.

The rationale behind the victims' rights movement was that crime victims should not be further harmed while in the process of seeking justice for the crimes committed against them. As a result of this movement, the last three or four decades have seen the creation of a number of resources, services, and protective measures for crime victims. Most cities or counties in the United States now have victim advocates who can assist, counsel, and support victims through the legal and personal processes following victimization. Many jurisdictions provide some funding to compensate crime victims, though budgets for such programs are relatively small. There are also psychologists and

The Central Park Jogger

In 1989, a 28 year old woman was running through New York City's Central Park, when she was brutally raped and beaten, then left to die. She was found four hours later, and though she was so severely injured that doctors predicted she would die, she eventually made a near complete recovery. Due to the horrific nature of the crime, the victim's identity was concealed. The assault on the jogger sparked such public outcry that it is seen as one of the critical factors that prompted an increasingly punitive response to criminal acts during the 1990s. The case focused on the idea that youthful offenders were engaging in rape and violence for the sheer enjoyment of such acts, something known as "wilding." Five young men were interrogated, confessed, and were convicted of the crimes. In 2002, another man already serving a life sentence for other crimes confessed to the 1989 crime, and DNA evidence corroborated his confession. The five men originally convicted were released, and their convictions were overturned on the assumption that their confessions had been coerced. In 2003, the victim went public and released a memoir called *I Am the Central Park Jogger: A Story of Hope and Possibility*. She now pursues a career as a motivational speaker.

Victim Impact Statements

A victim impact statement (VIS) is a written or oral testimonial delivered in court by a crime victim during the sentencing phase of a trial. In a VIS, victims can offer accounts of the effects that victimization have had on their lives; many victims outline both the physical and psychological trauma they experienced. In some jurisdictions, statements from mental health professionals are also admissible. In murder trials, a victim's family also can present a VIS. The widespread use of the VIS is an attempt to humanize the effects of the offender's crime, and to elevate the status of the victim within the criminal justice process. Victim impact statements can also be used during parole hearings, when convicted offenders are applying for early release from incarceration. Most states allow prosecuting attorneys to present VISs as testimony, even in death penalty cases.

counselors who specialize in helping victims of crime and trauma to cope with their experiences.

The victims' rights movement has also prompted changes in the criminal justice system itself. For example, law enforcement and court personnel now maintain higher standards in their interactions with victims, and these are specifically designed to avoid making the victim relive their trauma. Police now receive special training for handling cases involving rape and domestic violence, and many larger law enforcement agencies have specialized units that handle these cases. Hospitals are better equipped to process rape victims with dignity; those administering tests, examining victims, and collecting evidence are trained to ensure that victims are treated compassionately. During court proceedings, victims of all crimes are now treated with greater dignity, and new guidelines prevent defense attorneys from badgering victims while they are testifying. In the United States, victims are frequently allowed to testify about how their lives have been affected by the crimes that victimized them.

FAMILY AND INTIMATE VIOLENCE
Academic knowledge related to domestic or partner abuse, child abuse, elder abuse, and sexual abuse is generally derived from the combined scholarly and activist efforts to understand and improve the post-victimization experiences of victims. Given the personal nature of relationships between the offenders and victims in such cases, these forms of victimization merit special attention and will be examined here in some depth.

Domestic Violence
Domestic violence, also designated as domestic abuse, intimate-partner violence, and spousal abuse, refers to abusive behaviors, whether physical, sexual,

or verbal/psychological, within an intimate relationship such as a marriage, domestic partnership, or a dating relationship. It is estimated that only about one-third of all cases of domestic violence are reported to authorities and that domestic violence affects as much as one-tenth of the U.S. population. Research indicates that both males and females can be perpetrators and/or victims of domestic violence; however, the overwhelming majority of offenders are male, whereas the vast majority of victims are female. Domestic violence takes place in all forms of intimate relationships, including same-sex relationships. The abuse can be physical (e.g., causing pain or other bodily harm), emotional (e.g., causing psychological distress, humiliation, intimidation, or denying a person access to basic resources or privileges), financial (e.g., exploiting one's partner financially by controlling money or decisions about money), or sexual (e.g., coerced/forced engagement in undesirable, demeaning, or unsafe sex practices).

There are many theories regarding the causes of domestic violence. Sociologists suggest that domestic violence is more prevalent in households in which people are stressed because of their inability to secure adequate resources, particularly money. Others suggest that those who are exposed to domestic violence, particularly as children, are more likely to learn and adopt such behaviors later in life. Finally, some sociologists suggest that domestic violence is an expression of an offender's desire to exert or maintain power and control over a domestic partner. In cases of male-on-female domestic violence, such use of violence can also be interpreted as the desire to maintain traditional male privilege or dominance over women. In addition to the physical pain and suffering caused by domestic violence victimization, the victim also experiences forms of psychological and emotional trauma characteristic of all victims. However, victims of domestic violence may face even more severe forms of trauma, including homelessness and financial instability if the relationship dissolves, or a sense of self-blame and a damaged sense of intimacy, which makes it more difficult to form and maintain healthy relationships in the future.

In recent decades, knowledge about domestic violence has increased greatly, leading to widespread changes in public attitudes and policies. Research suggests that domestic violence is often a serial offense, likely to be repeated over time, and that the arrest of the offender is the single most effective quality in reducing the probability that the offense will be repeated. Given the oftentimes complex interpersonal relationship between offenders and victims in domestic violence cases, many victims are unwilling to pursue criminal charges against the offender, despite having initially called the police. As a result, many police agencies have developed mandatory arrest policies in cases of domestic-partner violence. In addition to criminal prosecution of the offenders in such cases, therapeutic approaches commonly include counseling for both offenders and victims.

Child Abuse

Child abuse most commonly involves the physical, psychological, or sexual abuse of a child by parents or other family members. It occurs in a variety of forms, including neglect (i.e., the child is denied physical, emotional, and medical care or attention) physical abuse (which involves inappropriate or excessive use of physical force), emotional abuse (including humiliation and imposition of inappropriate demands), and sexual abuse (i.e., in cases where an adult or older adolescent family member abuses the child for sexual gratification). The causes and effects of child abuse are similar to those of intimate-partner abuse, and sociologists have established a causal link between child abuse and other forms of familial violence. That is, those offenders who physically abuse their spouses are also more likely to abuse their children. In addition, there seems to be an association between substance abuse and child abuse.

What makes the issue of child abuse complicated is that we often lack widespread academic and social consensus of what constitutes abuse of children. For

Neglected child. *(Shutterstock)*

example, traditional parental discipline included the use of corporal punishment in child rearing, and those parents who did not use physical discipline were considered poor parents. However, as standards for appropriate parental discipline changed over time, attitudes about once acceptable degrees of physical punishment have also changed. Many parents use little or no physical force as a form of parental discipline, while many others have reduced the extent and frequency of physical discipline. In addition, resources on appropriate parenting skills are more readily available as are resources for children and others that provide information on where and how to report cases of suspected child abuse. In most counties in the United States, there are child protective services agencies, which investigate cases of alleged child abuse and neglect. If necessary, child protective service personnel are authorized to remove children from households where they are at risk and place them with foster families. Reports of child abuse can come from any source, including neighbors, family members, or even the children themselves. Teachers, school administrators, psychologists, and others who work with children are mandated to report suspected child abuse to authorities.

Elder Abuse

Elder abuse can include the same pattern of abuse observed in other forms of family violence—neglect, physical abuse, emotional abuse, overmedication, and sexual abuse. One common trend seen in cases of elder abuse is financial abuse, with abusers manipulating or intimidating or simply cheating an elderly person for personal financial gain. This may include misuse of funds and/or property, manipulating a power of attorney, and will tampering. Abusive caretakers have been known to deliberately place their elderly charges in harm's way by abandoning them in dangerous places or circumstances. Many abusers of elders are relatives, but abuse is also perpetrated by people who have been entrusted with caring for an elderly person or by trusted non-family members.

Studies suggest that about one in twenty older adults may be or have been subjected to some form of abuse or neglect. *(Shutterstock)*

Research in elder abuse is a growing field, and studies suggest that about one in twenty older adults may be have been subjected to some form of abuse or neglect. Of these, approximately 60 percent were subjected to psychological abuse, about 40 percent to financial abuse, about 12 percent to physical abuse, and 2 percent to sexual abuse. Elderly women are the most likely to be abused (70 percent of abuse cases), and the most common offenders are spouses/partners or adult children. As in the case of children, most counties in the United States have **adult protective services** agencies, which investigate cases of alleged elder abuse and neglect. If necessary, adult protective service personnel are able to remove seniors from situations where they are at risk and can provide resources for those seniors who wish to seek additional help. Reports of elder abuse can come from any source, including neighbors, family members, or the seniors themselves. In addition, a variety of professionals (e.g., hospital staff or workers at senior centers) may also report suspected elder abuse. Perhaps one of the most troubling aspects of elder abuse is that a subset of elderly victims may be particularly vulnerable because they suffer from cognitive impairments such as dementia or Alzheimer's disease. These victims may lack the cognitive ability to recognize their victimization and/or to report it to appropriate authorities.

SUMMARY

Sociological research has the potential to contribute to improvements in social life, but academic work in criminology and deviancy studies alone cannot bring about such changes—simply put, the knowledge gained through research must be applied if change is to occur. One group that aids this leap from academic knowledge to real-world application is applied researchers, who often investigate potential solutions to concrete problems. For the most part, however, it is activists who are responsible for effecting fundamental social change. This is especially true in the case of victimology and victim advocacy.

In previous decades, criminology focused on crime as a violation of the rights of the society as a whole; the rights of individual victims were considered irrelevant. This focus was not entirely misplaced because society as a whole can certainly be considered a victim of crime—after all, crime does breed fear and anxiety, diminished trust, and can be rather expensive in many ways. But in maintaining this focus, the criminal justice system functioned primarily to protect the general social interests. Moreover, the same system was engaged in the pursuit of objectivity, a noble goal with sometimes ignoble fallout as it worked more to ensure the ethical and legal treatment of offenders and seldom worked to ensure the same considerations to the victims of those offenders.

At times, it appeared that the criminal justice system was subjecting victims to **secondary victimization**, the mistreatment of crime victims that follows the initial victimization. This mistreatment included shaming, blaming, and mistreatment by medical personnel and by criminal justice personnel. In addition,

Restorative Justice

Restorative justice (sometimes also known as reparative justice) is a peacemaking approach to criminal justice that focuses on meeting the needs of criminal offenders and their victims. Such an approach is an alternative to the criminal justice system's relatively impersonal application of justice via punishment of offenders. Instead, restorative justice includes victims as active participants in the justice process, and its particular focus is on repairing the social relationships that have been damaged by a criminal event. Advocates of restorative justice encourage offenders to take responsibility for the damage they have caused by requiring them to apologize to victims, make amends for their wrong doings, engage in community service, and replace or repair damaged goods. The ultimate goal of restorative justice is to repair damaged social relations. In practice, however, it is often a difficult process because it requires offenders to take responsibility for their actions and the consequences of those actions for victims. In addition, the process requires participation (and sometimes forgiveness) by the victims, something that is difficult for many victims to confront.

victims of crimes were sometimes stigmatized, as in cases where an abuse victim was perceived at least partially to blame for the abuse.

The discipline of victimology has clarified some of these dynamics, and steps have been taken to reduce or remove those that re-victimize victims. Victim advocacy has grown into a strong social force, and more resources are now available for crime victims than ever before. The United States and many other nations have instituted laws preserving victims' rights, and scholarship in the area has increased greatly. On an international level, the United Nations has

Victim–Offender Reconciliation

Recent decades have seen the development of Victim–Offender Mediation Programs (VOMs) and Victim–Offender Reconciliation Programs (VORPs), which are designed to resolve differences between victims and their offenders. Such programs are completely voluntary for both parties, and allow victims and offenders to engage in peaceful dialogue in the presence of a trained mediator. The process allows victims to confront offenders about the physical and mental anguish offenders inflicted upon them and allow offenders to acknowledge the hurt, apologize, and offer to make amends. In the spirit of peacemaking and restoring harmony, VOMs and VORPs allow for individual-level reconciliation that has largely been irrelevant in the traditional practice of criminal justice.

Assistance for Victims of Crime and Abuse

Being a victim is of course a difficult experience (both for the victim and their loved ones), however there are resources available:

- In all cases, if you or someone else is in immediate danger of victimization or abuse, notify the police immediately by dialing 911.
- To report domestic violence, call 1-800-799-7233 and TTY 1-800-787-3224, or visit www.nnedv.org.
- To report suspected child abuse, dial 1-800-4-A-CHILD, or visit www.childhelp.org.
- To report suspected elder abuse, dial 1-800-677-1116, or visit http://www.ncea.aoa.gov.
- For more general assistance, search for your location here http://ovc.ncjrs.gov/findvictimservices/.

issued formal statements regarding the preservation of dignity and justice for crime victims. Those interested in restoring peace by fixing social relationships damaged by criminal events have also developed mediation and reconciliation programs. These new approaches go far beyond traditional conceptions of punishment and try to restore social relationships by addressing the hurt and damage experienced by victims.

Further Reading

Crosson-Tower, Cynthia. *Understanding Child Abuse and Neglect*, 8th ed. Boston, Mass.: Pearson Education, 2009.

McCue, Margi Laird. *Domestic Violence: A Reference Handbook*, 2nd ed. Santa Barbara, Calif.: ABC-CLIO, 2008.

Meili, Trisha. *I Am the Central Park Jogger: A Story of Hope and Possibility.* New York: Scribner, 2003.

National Center for Victims of Crime. Home page. http://www.ncvc.org.

Office of Justice Programs. Office for victims of crime. Available at http://www.ovc.com.

U.S. Administration on Aging. National Center on Elder Abuse home page. Available at http://www.ncea.aoa.gov.

U.S. Department of Health and Human Services for the Administration for Children and Families. Child welfare information gateway. Available at http://www.childwelfare.gov/.

Von Hentig, Hans. *The Criminal and his Victim: Studies in the Sociobiology of Crime.* New Haven: Yale University Press, 1948.

CHAPTER 5

DEVIANT LABELS
AND IDENTITIES

The concepts of deviant labels and identities have been consistent concerns for scholars engaged in crime and deviancy studies. One aspect of research related to deviant and criminal behaviors has revealed that patterns in deviant behaviors can mirror patterns in nondeviant behaviors. For example, just as a person can have a legitimate career that includes certain functions and responsibilities, a person can also have a career in crime or deviance, and this career also comes with functions and responsibilities. Thus, studying how people form deviant identities and careers, how they maintain these statuses, and how they exit these statuses is an important concern for scholars of deviance. Of particular interest is how deviant behaviors and persons are identified, as well as how those individuals labeled as deviants develop identities designed to correspond to those deviant labels, and even how such behaviors and identities are sometimes intertwined with body image. Each of these issues is discussed in this chapter.

LABELING AND DEVIANT IDENTITIES

Scholars of deviance approach their research by asking the following questions: How does a person become deviant? Why do others not become deviant? Criminologist Edwin Sutherland suggested that the distinction could be explained by **differential association**—a theory proposing that those who interacted more with deviant persons were more likely to adopt deviant attitudes and behaviors. Sutherland assumed that deviant behaviors and attitudes were learned (as opposed to innate), and that they were learned through social interaction with

Differential association posits that those who interact with deviant persons more than they interact with nondeviant persons are more likely to adopt deviant behaviors. *(Shutterstock)*

others who demonstrated deviant behaviors and/or held deviant belief systems. Sutherland further assumed that deviancy was learned via the same learning mechanisms through which people learn any other social behavior. This learning process, according to Sutherland, takes place within close social relationships, particularly family groups and peer groups. The underlying mechanism that determines whether a person engages in conformist or deviant behavior lies in that person's attitude toward social norms and conformity. A person who has been socialized in a manner that favors conformity follows the norms. A person who has been socialized in a manner that favor transgression against normative standards engages in deviant behavior.

As a learned behavior, deviant conduct involves a variety of technical and psychological tools, including methods, attitudes, and neutralizations. In other words, the individual must learn how to engage in deviant behaviors. Such behaviors may be simple, such as shoplifting by placing merchandise in one's pocket, or they may be highly complicated, such as methods for conducting elaborate banking fraud. Either way, these behaviors are learned in the social environment either through trial and error or more commonly as part of a complex process through which a person is socialized into deviance. In addition to the physical techniques associated with deviance, the acquisition of beliefs favoring norm transgression means that the deviant individual acquires a set of convictions that positively value deviance. As an emotional tool to managing potentially stigmatizing actions, the deviant person learns to interpret conformist behavior(s) negatively at the same time as he or she learns to interpret norm-breaking behavior positively. In connection with this, deviant cultures and subcultures develop **techniques of neutralization**, rationalizations which justify deviant behavior and which are used to help deviant persons maintain a positive view about violating norms of the broader culture.

Labeling and Stigma

Although differential association theory helps to clarify how a person enters deviance, it does not as strongly clarify how social responses from others play a role in creating deviance. This ambiguity about the impact of social responses allows us to consider the possibility that it is not the inherent qualities of many acts which make them deviant, but rather the creation of social rules and their enforcement that makes behaviors deviant. Some sociologists suggest that people become deviant when they violate the social rules (which we assume they did not create) and when they are labeled as deviant by those who created the rules or uphold them as correct and appropriate norms. Therefore, the social reaction to norm-breaching behaviors has everything to do with *creating* deviance.

Sociologist Howard Becker is known as the field's foremost proponent of **labeling theory**, which is the idea that deviance is defined by the social identification of behaviors, persons, and attitudes deemed socially undesirable, and therefore through the application of negative labels. In his 1963 book *Outsiders* Becker wrote

> *Social groups create deviance by making rules whose infraction constitutes deviance,* and by applying those roles to particular people and labeling them as outsiders. From this point of view, deviance is *not* a quality of the act the person commits, but rather a consequence of the application by others of rules

and sanctions to an "offender." The deviant is one to whom that label has been successfully applied; deviant behavior is behavior that people so label.

From this perspective, it is not merely a behavioral violation of norms that matters for the deviance process, but also the fact that it is socially identified and defined as deviant.

The idea that social reactions to behavior are crucial to defining certain behaviors, persons, and attitudes as undesirable or wrong is important for understanding the socially constructed nature of deviance. Labeling theory describes the reflexive process that occurs between rule transgressors and those who respond to those transgressions; however, the process is not always fair and equitable. Consider that one individual may carry out a secret career of deviance for a long time, during which time those behaviors might not be identified. In the case of secret deviance, such as private illicit drug use, an individual will not be identified as deviant, and therefore will not be subject to negative

Techniques of Neutralization

In the classic 1964 study *Delinquency and Drift*, Matza examined the process through which those engaged in deviance maintained positive self-images. The study found that deviant persons often feel pressures to conform and may feel guilty after violating norms. To ameliorate the pressures and guilt, norm violators learned to employ a number of techniques of neutralization to help them maintain a positive outlook toward themselves and their behaviors.

- *Denial of responsibility.* Offenders claim they were forced into a situation or were unable to control themselves: "They made me do it." Or, "I couldn't help myself."
- *Denial of injury.* Offenders claim their behaviors do not cause any damage or injury: "Nobody gets hurt."
- *Denial of the victim.* Offenders claim the victims deserved to be victimized: "They were asking for it." or "They had it coming to them."
- *Condemning the condemners.* Offenders criticize those accusing them of wrongdoing by pointing out that the accusers are just as bad or worse: "If you think we're bad, then you should see the things they do." Or, "They're just trying to shift their own blame onto us."
- *Appeals to higher loyalties.* Offenders justify their actions by pointing out that they were in pursuit of higher goals and principles: "You have to protect your friends, even if it means you have to break some rules." Or, "You just have to break some rules; otherwise you could never get anything done."

The Scarlet Letter

The 1850 novel *The Scarlet Letter* written by Nathaniel Hawthorne is a well-known example of the use of social stigma to indicate moral dishonor. The book is set in 17th-century Puritan Massachusetts, and the main character is Hester Prynne, a woman who is socially condemned for conceiving a child in an extramarital affair. As part of her punishment, Hester must wear a red piece of cloth in the shape of the letter A, which indicates her disgraced social status as an adulteress. Throughout the book, Hester struggles with her guilt while searching for redemption.

The Scarlet Letter is widely read in American literature classes, and the novel has been reproduced as a motion picture (several different versions). Because the story deals directly and literally with the stigmatization process, it is considered a classic tale for understanding the labeling process and the consequences of social stigma.

social consequences from the behavior. However, another person might engage in similar behaviors and be observed while doing so. This person could then be labeled as deviant and even be subjected to informal and formal sanctions. Note that the fundamental difference lies not in the acts themselves (which are the same), but in whether the acts have been witnessed and the subsequent social reaction (or lack of reaction) to those acts. A corollary to this is that someone who is not responsible for a deviant act may nonetheless be labeled as deviant if that person is perceived to be responsible for an act, regardless of the veracity of that claim. A good example is how rumors can damage someone's social standing or status, even if they are untrue.

Sociologist Erving Goffman popularized the concept of stigma, which is the idea that those who have been labeled as deviant carry a **social stigma**, a condition that invites negative social labels that affects that person's identity and inhibit normalcy in social interactions. Stigma, a word of Greek origin, was originally used to refer to a mark that was tattooed or branded on the skin of a person deemed to be criminal or immoral. Though some stigma may be physical in nature, such as physical marks or special clothing, social stigma are more commonly symbolic in nature and may include disavowal, disapproval, or attribution of membership to an undesirable group.

Socially, stigma facilitates the functioning of a number of social mechanisms. Stigma differentiates between groups and clarifies in-group and out-group statuses. Stigma can also evoke stereotypes or trigger social control responses. In addition, once assumed or applied, stigma can be difficult to live down and often has a lasting effect on the lives of those who have been stigmatized. A tarnished reputation, for example, can be very difficult to live down. Also consider the difficulties facing an ex-convict trying to find a job or rent a house having to fill out applications that inevitably inquire about felony convictions.

Stages of Deviance and Identity Development

As explained above, people cannot be stigmatized unless their negative attributes are recognized by others. When embarking on a career of deviance, many individuals initially hide their misdeeds. In the initial stages, known as **primary deviance**, deviant acts remain hidden. Because it is not recognized by others, primary deviance has little or no effect on the self-identity and social standing of the person practicing the behavior. Concealing illicit drug use or masking a preference for same-sex relationships are examples of primary deviance. The associated behaviors are **discreditable**, meaning they can be outwardly concealed. Other forms of deviance are known as **discredited**, which means that they are either not concealable or that they have been discovered by or revealed to others.

Once deviant behavior is revealed and recognized, it becomes **secondary deviance**. In this stage deviant behaviors or statuses are recognized and subjected to social control responses. Typically, the deviance is labeled, and the person committing the deviant act may also be labeled. Others may also engage in a retrospective analysis of the deviant's past behavior, in which past actions are reexamined in light of the newly identified deviant acts or statuses. In the secondary stage, the deviant individual may take on a deviant **master status**, the primary identifying social characteristic of an individual, whether ascribed or achieved. The master status tends to eclipse all other social characteristics of that person, and others begin to interact with that person predominantly via that characteristic. If, for example, someone's master status is "ex-convict," others will likely view that individual through their perception of that attribute. And although this ex-convict may have a variety of attributes as a person, the single attribute of having been convicted of a crime dominates as that person's social identity.

When individuals are assigned a deviant master status, they are clearly subject to external social consequences. But this labeling, however, may also have internal consequences and affect a person's self-image. In the secondary deviance stage, many stigmatized individuals also develop a **deviant identity**, which means that they may adopt the attitudes and practices associated with the stigmatized role now attributed to them. As this secondary deviance process continues, they may also increase their involvement and commitment to deviant groups and behaviors. This occurs as they begin to see themselves through the deviant role identity. Thus, the application of a deviant label may be a self-fulfilling prophecy because the adoption of a particular label as a salient identity can lead to the amplification of the associated deviance.

Erving Goffman's *Asylums*

In 1961, Erving Goffman published his classic work *Asylums: Essays on the Social Situation of Mental Patients and Other Inmates.* The book was based on Goffman's observations inside a mental hospital, during which time Goffman took extensive field notes about various aspects of patient life. Goffman focused heavily on the process through which patients were admitted to the mental hospital (i.e., institutionalized) and how order was maintained within the institution. In his book, Goffman coined the term "total institution," which is still used to describe the type of institution that controls all aspects of an inmate's life. (Examples of total institutions include mental hospitals, prisons, and the military.)

One of the principal arguments in Goffman's book was that the rules in the mental hospital often had more to do with the staff's efforts to maintain control than it did with curing the conditions that had put patients in the mental institution. Thus, one goal within a total institution is compliance, and at the institution in question, this goal often was at odds with efforts to treat psychiatric disorders. While the therapeutic practices in present-day mental hospitals may have evolved, Goffman's *Asylums* is still widely read in sociology classes studying mental illness, deviance, and criminology.

Individuals who belong to powerful groups are better able to defend themselves against stigmatization than are the members of disempowered groups, who are more often subjected to the efforts of other groups to define their behaviors. For example, medical practitioners and business executives are relatively empowered groups, and despite the fact that some members of these groups might engage in illegal activities, the members of the group as a whole maintain a positive image in the general public perception. In contrast, members of disempowered groups may not be able to resist labeling and therefore may be subjected more sharply to negative labeling.

In recent years, some disempowered groups have embraced their stigmatized labels, using them as political tools. This part of the process is known as **tertiary deviance** and is exemplified by groups that have learned to value their negative images and use the associated stigmas to advocate their own interests or those of others who have been labeled deviant. For example, a number of prostitutes have organized a group known as COYOTE (which stands for Call off Your Old Tired Ethics). COYOTE members advocate on behalf of the interests of illegal sex workers, arguing that sex work should be legalized and regulated just like any legitimate industry.

Finally, some deviants exit their careers, whether the duration of their involvement is short or extended. One major hurdle that such individuals confront is

The Professional Ex

One interesting option for transmuting a deviant career into a normal career is to become what is known as a "professional ex." Sociologist J. David Brown suggested that a large number of people have exited deviant careers by becoming counselors or experts dealing with exiting deviant careers. For example, a large number of drug and alcohol counselors have themselves been former substance abusers. Becoming a professional ex may happen through a systematic process, in which those wishing to stop deviant behaviors begin imitating the behavior of their counselors, ultimately adopting the normative behaviors and attitudes they emulated. The idea of the professional ex has generated some controversy, because some sociologists argue that the role is an extension of a deviant career, while others suggest that the switch to the professional ex role represents a desistance of deviant behavior.

living down the stigma associated with the deviant role. One major goal is to adopt a conforming master status. The process varies from person to person, but most individuals reject or suppress their deviant behaviors and attitudes in an effort to appear outwardly conforming; in the process, they may also become inwardly conforming. The true shift occurs when someone shirks the deviant label both internally and socially and engages in developing or maintaining a normative social persona. This is not as difficult as it may seem because deviant persons often have one foot in the normative world despite living a deviant career. In practice, the line between conformity and deviance is permeable, and many people move back and forth between deviancy and normality, indeed in both directions. Without a doubt, a great number of people within any society have at one point or another engaged in some deviant behaviors; an equally large proportion of society has also exited deviance.

DEVIANCE AND BODY IMAGES

All persons are embodied, and therefore the physical presence of the body is relevant in all social interactions, and particularly so in face to face interactions. Therefore, forms of deviance relating to the body can be important for how a person's behavior is socially interpreted and for how a person interprets his or her own self-identity. All societies maintain standards for what is considered a **normal body image**, a term that defines the sense of what is an appropriate or desirable size, shape, or appearance of a body. But normal body image also refers to the way a person's body is viewed (favorably or unfavorably) in relation to those standards. Body attributes are particularly important in relation to deviancy studies because many physical attributes are ascribed, and most are obvious traits that cannot be disavowed. In discussing deviant body images that may carry social stigma, this section explores two deviant behaviors: body modification and eating disorders.

Body modification is the intentional alteration of the physical body for nonmedical purposes, which may include religious expression, self-adornment/ aesthetics, rites of passage, indications of group membership, or shock value.

Tattoos mark the face of Tukukino, a Ngāti Tamaterā chief. *(Wikipedia)*

Some forms of body modification are commonplace and socially accepted (e.g., ear piercing of females in many cultures) or even religiously mandated (e.g., circumcision of males in some traditions). Other forms are accepted in moderation, but may be condemned if extreme (e.g., tattooing, body piercing, hair removal and/or growth, intentional development of muscles, gaining and/or losing weight, and cosmetic surgeries such as breast augmentation and facelifts). Some forms of body modification are considered aesthetically pleasing or acceptable within certain cultural contexts, although they are controversial or outright rejected outside those contexts. Some traditional societies, for example, have practiced foot binding in females, extensive tattooing and/or scarification, neck stretching in women, corseting to maintain narrow waists, stretching of lips or ear lobes, and genital cutting. Within those cultures, the practices are typically intended to enhance appearance; other cultures may find some or all of these practices barbaric and/or unsightly.

In modern societies, there are also those who engage in extensive body modification because they are involved in subcultures of body modification. Known as "primitives," such individuals pursue body modification to an extent that is well outside mainstream expectations and acceptance (i.e., all over their bodies, including faces and genitals). Body modification has generated controversy, which stems from a lack of agreement about what is and is not aesthetically pleasing. While proponents of extreme body modification suggest that

Female Genital Cutting

Also known as female circumcision and female genital mutilation, female genital cutting (FGC) has become increasingly controversial as a social issue related to body modification. FCG involves the partial or total removal of external female genitals, including the clitoris and vaginal labia. The practice is most widespread in North Africa, the Middle East, and Southeast Asia, though it is also practiced among some immigrant groups in North America and Europe. The motivations for the practice involve traditional sensibilities related to culture and religion, the preservation of virginity and sexual purity for young girls, and enhancing the marriageability of a young woman. According to the World Health Organization (WHO) (the health authority within the United Nations), there is no health benefit to FGC, and the practice may lead to a number of health problems, including urinary tract infections, infertility, complications in childbirth, psychological distress, and loss of genital sensitivity. The WHO estimates that an estimated 100 to 140 million girls and women have undergone FCG, mostly in African nations. The WHO recognizes FGC as a violation of human rights and is engaged in efforts to study FGC in an ongoing effort to stop the practice worldwide.

their practices enhance beauty, critics suggest that extreme modifications are a form of disfigurement. Indeed, those engaged in extensive body modification are sometimes diagnosed with a psychological disorder known as body dysmorphic disorder, a condition characterized by excessive concern about some perceived defect in physiology.

Dieting to gain or lose weight has long been an important cultural strain in Western societies, and whole industries have developed around the practice of dieting and the fads associated with it. While dieting may be considered normative in Western cultures, there are those who take this body modification practice to pathological extremes. **Eating disorders** are defined as unconventional food consumption practices, the most common of which involve eating too little or eating too much. In the United States, it is estimated that approximately 8 million persons suffer from eating disorders. Although most individuals with eating disorders are female, about 10 percent are male. The best known eating disorders are **anorexia nervosa** (cases in which a person eats an insufficient amount of food to sustain the body and is highly averse to gaining weight) and **bulimia nervosa** (cases in which a person binges on food, and then engages in purging via vomiting and/or taking laxatives).

There are of course some biological and psychological/personality correlates to eating disorders, but culture is a critical factor. U.S. culture in particular tends to value being in control of one's body, and many people interpret nonstandard body weight as the result of individual irresponsibility. Contemporary culture may thus exert a high degree of social pressure on individuals to maintain what is perceived to be a normal weight and may inadvertently promote eating disorders as a way to accomplish this.

Deviance Processes and the Body

Every person has a body, and practices relating to body image are fundamental to social interactions. Therefore, violations of body image norms influence not only how others react to a person's behaviors but also how persons form and maintain self-identity. Norms about body image are socially learned; ironically, so are the techniques and attitudes necessary for violating those norms. We find, for example, that those who violate norms associated with body image often associate with others who do the same, and those who engage in extreme body modification do so within a subculture that values such modifications. Thus, the principle of differential association holds true.

Deviance, as explained earlier in this chapter, is an evolutionary process. If carried out in secret, the stage of primary deviance persists and may even bring positive social rewards, as in the example of weight control achieved via pathological eating behaviors. Ironically, while such methods of controlling weight may be condemned if detected, the results of maintaining a healthy weight may be positively rewarded. Hidden forms of deviant body images can of course be discreditable; other forms are detectable and can be immediately discredited. Thus, body modifications in the stage of secondary deviance may be judged and labeled negatively by the wider society, and a negative social stigma may be applied to those who practice nonmainstream body modification.

As an example, obesity is something which cannot be concealed, and in a social sense becomes immediately obvious in face-to-face interactions. In past centuries, obesity was considered desirable and an indication of status and wealth. In contemporary Western cultures, obesity is often stigmatized, even though it is formally defined as a medical condition. Recent decades have also seen the rise of a grassroots effort to change social attitudes toward obese and overweight persons. The existence of the this "fat acceptance movement" (FAM) suggests tertiary deviance as obese persons learn to value their body image and are using this to advocate their own interests and refute the negative stigma borne by those who are overweight.

SUMMARY
Sociologists of crime and deviancy continue to examine issues of labeling, stigma, and deviant identity development. The deviance process is dynamic and evolves over time, a process that involves the interaction of deviant individuals and groups as well as the reactions of society as a whole. On the one hand, deviant individuals learn the practices and attitudes necessary to carry out their behaviors or lifestyles; on the other hand, society reacts to detectable forms of deviance by applying labels and social stigma. In some instances, those considered deviant by the standards of mainstream society and culture are embracing the deviance and refuting the negative stigma imposed on them by others.

Further Reading

Fumento, Michael. *The Fat of the Land: The Obesity Epidemic and How Overweight Americans Can Help Themselves*. New York: Viking, 1997.

Gary, Jason, and Greg Jacobson (producers). *Modify*. Committed Films, 2006. DVD, 85 minutes.

Goffman, Erving. *Asylums: Essays on the Social Situation of Mental Patients and Other Inmates*. New York: Anchor Books, 1961.

Matza, David. *Delinquency and Drift*. New York: John Wiley and Sons, Inc., 1964.

National Eating Disorders Association. Welcome page. Available at http://www.nationaleatingdisorders.org/.

Pitts, Victoria. *In the Flesh: The Cultural Politics of Body Modification*. New York: Palgrave Macmillan, 2003.

World Health Oranization. Eliminating female genital mutilation. Available at http://www.who.int/reproductivehealth/publications/fgm/9789241596442/en/index.html

World Health Organization. Female genital mutilation and other harmful practices. Available at http://www.who.int/reproductivehealth/topics/fgm/en/index.html.

CHAPTER 6

SUBCULTURES AND SUBCULTURAL STUDIES

For the past few decades, subcultural studies have been an area of much interest in sociology, anthropology, cultural studies, and other related disciplines. A **subculture** is a group of people (overt or covert) whose norms and values differ from those of the mainstream culture. Although all subcultures, by definition, may deviate from the dominant norms of the broader culture in which they exist, not all are considered undesirable. In fact, some subcultures may be considered deviant because their actions, philosophies, and perhaps even appearance might be positive examples of things that the norms of the dominant society may resist, admire, or even aspire to emulate. A detailed look at positive deviance is covered in Chapter 8; for the purposes of this chapter on subcultures, we will focus predominantly on those groups which are considered deviant in the sense that their unwillingness or inability to conform to typical societal expectations makes members of the broader society view them as undesirable or odd or aberrant.

Urban youth gangs, for example, are a type of criminal subculture whose members live according to criminal norms, and whose sense of what is appropriate differs greatly from what the society at large deems appropriate. The Amish are also a subculture, and though they are far from criminal, their lifestyle, which eschews the use of modern technologies, also sets them apart from the broader culture. The Amish are an example of a **fringe subculture**, a term that describes subcultures that avoid interactions with those in mainstream society. A **counterculture** is a special type of subculture whose norms directly

Hippie Counterculture

One of the most famous countercultures in the United States was the hippie culture of the 1960s and 1970s. This countercultural movement, populated almost entirely by young people, was characterized by its rejection of the traditional values of the 1950s and in particular, for its opposition to racial segregation and the Vietnam War. Hippies rejected traditional notions of material success and the American Dream and therefore opposed traditional forms of authority, such as the police and the military, as well as traditional concepts of what was appropriate and socially acceptable. Hippies favored peaceful social relations, racial integration, gender equality, freedom of sexual expression, and experimenting with drugs. The hippie culture peaked in the late 1960s and then faded, arguably because of mainstream society's scorn for its characteristic pleasure-seeking lifestyle and overt drug abuse. Contemporary remnants of the hippie counterculture include cultural artifacts such as psychedelic music and images, hippie clothing, and hippie hairstyles. On more concrete levels, the hippies contributed to social movements bringing the Vietnam War to an end and advancing civil rights in the United States.

conflict with the norms of the mainstream society. Countercultural groups espouse and live by values that openly contradict the commonly held values in a society.

THE SOCIAL UTILITY OF SUBCULTURES

Subcultures emerge and persist in part because they help their members negotiate the challenges of social life. Sociologist Michael Brake, in his book *The Sociology of Youth and Youth Subcultures*, argues that subcultures assist their members in five important aspects of social life. To begin with, subcultures are problem-solving groups, which help their members to confront challenges, whether those challenges are material or existential. For example, the values and practices espoused by members of criminal subcultures might help individuals to provide for their material needs, whereas other subcultures might answer existential questions related to the meaning of life and clarify an individual's relationship to a given social group and to society at large. Some religious subcultures, for example, might provide their members with answers relating to the meaning of life, and thereby offer a purpose to life.

Secondly, membership in subcultures can make social experiences more manageable. Social life can be very complex, and many individuals are marginalized (or at least feel excluded) from social interactions in the mainstream. By providing an alternate set of beliefs and practices in social interaction, membership in a subculture can make social interactions more predictable. Entering and maintaining social relationships may be difficult in all areas of social life, but this difficulty is particularly evident in adolescent social circles, which may be one reason many young people gravitate toward subcultural groups.

According to Brake, a third benefit subcultures can provide is an alternate systems of meaning and reality. Highly developed subcultures typically have highly developed sets of symbols that are used to communicate and define deeper, more abstract concepts of life and exert an influence on the psyche of those experiencing the subculture. In its extreme form, these symbols can create an alternate reality system for its members. For example, religious cults are examples of subcultures which create alternate realities for their members, and frequently these alternate realties fall outside of what are considered conventional interpretations of reality. For example, many in Evangelical Christian circles use the letters WWJD, which is short for "What Would Jesus Do?" as a short-hand to evoke Christian perspectives in social life. In other, more earthbound, subcultures, extensive use of symbols in fashion, music, or jargon can serve a similar purpose and provide a sense of belonging. For example, membership in youth cliques are often defined ostensibly via fashion cues (like hair or clothing styles), participation in leisure pursuits, and preference for a certain genre of pop music.

Brake's fourth point is that subcultures can help to define or structure leisure time. Skateboarders, for example, are members of a subculture that centers on a well-recognized form of recreation. Although skateboarding has been a leisure activity for many decades, it is only in recent decades that skateboarding has emerged as a distinctly leisure-based subculture. Skate subcultures continue to center on the leisure pursuit of skateboarding, but many skateboarders now share strikingly uniform clothes, hairstyles, video games, musical genres, and slang. Another example of a leisure/recreational subculture involves diehard fans of a pop cultural phenomenon (e.g., a TV show or a musical group) to such an extent that the phenomenon becomes salient to their sense of self-identity. The nature of the phenomenon varies from soccer to soap operas to country music and beyond, but at the core of each pop culture subculture is a fan identity that is shared with other fans with the same interest(s).

Finally, Brake defines subcultures as social spaces where individuals can work out personal issues, and particularly where they can engage in identity seeking. Finding one's place in social relations is important, especially for youth, but indeed for anyone, because individuals who do not feel integrated or included in social relations often feel lost or isolated. Membership in one or more subcultures can provide a much-needed sense of belonging, which in turn provides a stable basis for negotiating self-identity and relations to the social environment. Because forming a self-identity of any kind is a phenomenon experienced by all young people, much of the focus of subcultural studies has been on youth involvement in subcultures.

Style and Subcultures

The use of **style cues** (symbolic images in fashion, pop culture, and argot, often employed to communicate membership both to insiders and outsiders) is an important aspect of subcultures and therefore an important focus of subcultural studies. An example of the kinds of things that such studies observe can be easily illustrated through an examination of a single subculture. Punk rockers, for example, can be identified by the clothes they wear (e.g., dark boots and ripped jeans), distinctive hairstyles (e.g., Mohawk haircuts and unusual coloration of hair), and their musical taste. The punk rock subculture has been characterized by its association with punk music, a style characterized by its rapid pace, simple instrumentation, short songs, antiestablishment lyrics, and for its noncommercial production. Peaking in the late 1970s, the punk counterculture was often seen as opposing the excessive lifestyles adopted by mainstream rock groups in the early 1970s. Despite the punk rock culture's decline, its cultural influence of punk rock can still be seen in subsequent subcultural movements including New Wave, Alternative Rock, Goth, and Emo, all of which are subcultures defined to a great extent by their relation to musical genres and style cues.

Member of the punk rock subculture. *(Shutterstock)*

Many subcultures (and their members) are initially identified through their distinctive symbols. Over time, however, the identification process may be blurry, especially if subculture style cues filter into the mainstream culture and are adopted and used for other purposes. Corporate interests, for instance, often recognize the cultural appeal of subcultural images and therefore adopt and use them as marketing tools or as marketworthy offerings. One example of this phenomenon is the gangster rap clothing now widely produced and marketed to a mass market that reaches well beyond the subculture originally associated with the style. The same phenomenon has occurred with music. Many genres of music (including jazz, rock, hip hop, and grunge) were once considered shocking. Today such music is well-integrated into

Dick Hebdige's *Subculture: The Meaning of Style*

Published in 1979, this book has become a classic in cultural studies and subcultural studies on crime and deviance. Drawing on earlier work regarding the use of symbols to communicate meaning, Hebdige argued that members of subcultures indicate their association via symbolic styles, including clothing styles, hairstyles, gestures, and slang. *Subculture* offers a history of the punk rock subculture, and although the veracity of the history itself has been questioned, the book is important because the author situated the punk movement in its historic and cultural contexts. Hebdige argued that punk rock did not simply grow out of thin air; rather, he argued that the movement was historically rooted in 1970s white British working class youth opposition to the values espoused by their parents' generation and to pressures in the job market brought on by immigration. Thus, Hebdige argues that the punkers assembled a variety of symbols (including fashion and music) that communicated their opposition to the dominant culture of the time, which they perceived as a repressive impediment to their future life chances.

mainstream culture and heard almost everywhere. Indeed, many contemporary pluralistic societies seem to have the capacity to co-opt a wide variety of subcultures rather quickly. In some cases, cultural images that may initially seem threatening to mainstream values quickly become less threatening and commonplace; for cultural images that are not threatening to begin with, this co-opting is even easier.

Many subcultures are seen as innocuous and are tolerated from the start as being strange but harmless. For example, groups based on interests such as the science fiction television and film series *Star Trek*, professional wrestling, Civil War reenactments, recreational running, or baseball card collecting are easily tolerated, even though each is a subculture. Other subcultures, which are seen from the start as dangerous or too contrary to mainstream norms are never assimilated. Among these subcultures are racist skinhead groups, neo-Nazi groups, and urban criminal gangs. In fact, such virulent groups often attract the attention of criminal justice personnel who track and monitor their activities both for law enforcement purposes and for the purpose of understanding how these groups contribute to the wider crime problem. In extreme cases, dangerous style cues (e.g., gang symbols like tattoos, hand signs, and specific types of clothing) may be prohibited by mainstream institutions. Students in many urban high schools, for example, are prohibited from wearing clothing associated with criminal gangs. On a proactive level, police and prison systems often catalog gang symbols so they can identify gang members in the system. Using

Gang tatoo. *(Wikipedia)*

these cataloged symbols, prison authorities can avoid placing rival gang members in the same cells or other confined areas where conflict might erupt.

SUBCULTURES AND DEVIANT BELIEFS

Whereas many subculture studies focus on style cues, these are mainly surface indications that the groups identified by those symbols may hold deviant beliefs. Arguably, a more salient aspect of deviancy studies is that many deviant groups may be defined not simply by what they do or the style cues they adopt, but also by what they believe. **Deviant beliefs** are values or attitudes that are not accepted by mainstream society, and though they may be accepted in some subcultural circles, they are generally considered odd, undesirable, or repugnant. Examples of deviant beliefs include white supremacy, belief in UFO abductions, and environmental extremism. On an ideological level, many subcultures do indeed espouse values and beliefs that vary from the culture at large. To the extent that these values conflict with mainstream values, a subculture may be viewed as problematic to the wider society in which it exists. Clearly criminal subcultures have values which, by virtue of their violation of social standards such as codified by law, conflict directly with the interests of mainstream society. This section explores two varieties of subcultural beliefs: those that run directly counter to mainstream values (as exemplified by white supremacists and religious cults) and those that may differ from mainstream values, but which are tolerated by the society at large (as exemplified by those who believe in paranormal activities).

Countercultures and Deviant Beliefs

White supremacy is an extreme form of racial bias or ethnocentrism, which is the belief that one's own group is superior to all others. Frequently, white supremacy translates into antiblack or anti-Semitic behaviors, and white supremacy movements have been observed in a variety of countries with significant white populations, including those in North America, Europe, Latin America, southern Africa, Australia, and New Zealand. White supremacy is an example of **supremacism** in general, a term that refers to the belief that one's own group is superior to others. Supremacism extends beyond racial identity, and therefore supremacists believe that their own race, color, religion, language, culture, nation, sexual orientation, or other belief system is superior to all others. Supremacism is ironically color-blind and not exclusively the turf of white supremacist groups; there are also black supremacists and Asian supremacists.

Historically, white supremacy has been an official practice by some government agencies. In the 19th century, for example, slavery was legal and there were laws that prohibited marriage between races and prevented nonwhites from voting. Some parts of the United States practiced segregation in schools and other public institutions until the late 1960s, and South Africa practiced legal segregation under a system called apartheid until the 1990s. Though not positively sanctioned by governments, white supremacy has been widely practiced by a variety of groups. In the United States, the Ku Klux Klan (the KKK) is the group most closely associated with white supremacy. Originally created as an antiblack movement, the KKK has expanded its supremacist bias to anti-immigration, anti-Communism, and anti-Semitism. KKK members are best known for wearing conical white hats and white sheets, and for burning crosses at their rallies. The KKK has a history of terror, intimidation, and violence and is currently monitored as a hate group.

Many religious cults also espouse countercultural beliefs. A **religious cult** is a spiritual group whose practices and beliefs are considered strange by conventional religious standards. Some scholars argue that religious cults are new religious movements that should be tolerated and studied like any other social movement, although critics of cults counter that many are authoritarian in structure, exploitative of their members, and potentially dangerous both to cult members and to the society at large. Unlike sects of established religions, which typically emerge(d) from religious rifts, cults seem to focus on novel beliefs that have little or no connection with conventional religious ideologies. Cults are considered deviant groups because their beliefs fall outside conventional

Ku Klux Klan parade. *(Library of Congress)*

spiritual cultures; as a result, many cults generate a strong tension between their members and those who adhere to more traditionally accepted religious beliefs. At times, the label "cult" is used pejoratively by established religious groups to describe groups whose beliefs conflict with traditional, established religious groups and their beliefs. On the other hand, the term is also applied to new religious movements that are considered dangerous, especially those that involve arcane rituals and are led by a charismatic leader. Cults often generate strong opposition because they are generically associated with the few horrific cults that are deservedly infamous for their connection to brutal murders and suicide pacts.

Most critics of religious cults believe that cult organizations utilize brainwashing techniques to maintain the loyalty of their members, although the veracity of this claim is questioned by some social scientists. Those who oppose religious cults often cite the necessity to deprogram former cult members to rid them of brainwashing and resocialize them. In the past three or four decades, a number of cults have attracted a great deal of mass media attention, particularly centering on high-profile cases such as the mass suicides at Jonestown and the Manson Family murders.

Although it is true that some cults have been damaging to their members and to the communities in which they operate, many cults are relatively benign. Recognizing this distinction, scholars in religious studies have suggested the need to distinguish between new and alternative forms of spiritual practices and more dangerous forms of belief. Nonetheless, many countries (e.g., France, Italy, Belgium, Sweden, and China) have instituted policies that ban fringe religious practices, some of which are practiced openly in other countries (e.g., Falun Gong and Scientology). In contrast, the United States views the right to practice the religion of one's choosing as a legally protected right accorded to all, and does not prohibit or restrict religious cults as long as they do not violate any existing laws. Indeed, cults are now a part of popular culture, although media portrayals may not be entirely accurate. A noted example would be the book

Jim Jones and the Mass Suicide in Guyana

In 1978, more than 900 members of a religious cult known as the Peoples Temple, under the leadership of charismatic leader Jim Jones, committed suicide by drinking a grape-flavored drink laced with cyanide. In the early 1970s Jones had formed a religious cult aimed at creating a socialist utopia, and in 1974 the group began constructing a community at Jonestown, Guyana, in South America. By 1976, Jones and many of his followers had moved to Guyana to occupy Jonestown. Two years later, Jones and the Peoples Temple were under investigation by the U.S. government, which sent a delegation of officials to Guyana to investigate the group. The investigators were attacked by Peoples Temple members; a U.S. Congressman and several other members of the delegation were killed. After this attack, Jones felt that the movement was under attack by the U.S. government and advised his followers to commit suicide. The adults first poisoned over 270 children, and then poisoned themselves. Jones was found dead from a gunshot wound consistent with self-inflicted wounds. The mass suicide at Jonestown was responsible for the second-highest death toll of Americans in history (excluding deaths by natural disaster, epidemic, or war), second only to the death toll resulting from the terrorist attacks of September 11, 2001.

and film *The da Vinci Code*, which includes a skewed portrayal of the Roman Catholic group Opus Dei.

An example of a subculture that is relatively benign, and perhaps even widely accepted, is the belief in paranormal activities, which include such phenomena as witchcraft, psychic powers, astrology, prophecy, ghosts, numerology, creationism, séances, time travel, crop circles, Sasquatch, the Bermuda Triangle, and UFO abductions. In his book *Paranormal Beliefs*, sociologist Erich Goode defines **paranormal beliefs** as the belief in the veracity of phenomena that are both unlikely and scientifically unverifiable. Although paranormal phenomena, by definition, cannot be verified, what can be sociologically verified is that some people believe that these phenomena exist. In contemporary society, scientific study has become the predominant form of understanding all phenomena, yet belief in the paranormal nonetheless persists. In fact, despite the absence of verifiable facts to prove the existence of the supernatural, paranormal beliefs continue to flourish, as indicated by the broad marketing of books, videos, and Internet sites about the paranormal.

Crop Circles

Visible from the air, crop circles are patterns formed in fields by flattening crops such as wheat or corn. The term crop circle is a misnomer, as most crop circles are not round; they may in fact be quite elaborate in shape. Crop circles began appearing in the 1970s, and have appeared with increasing frequency since that time. The vast majority of crop circles have been sighted in the southern region of England, and particularly in areas where ancient ruins (such as Stonehenge) are found. A scientific investigation into crop circles conducted in 1999 and 2000 determined that 80 percent of crop circles could verifiably be traced to human origins, although the origin of the remaining 20 percent was unclear. Over the past few decades, various persons and organizations have claimed responsibility for crop circles, and many companies have paid to have crop circles created for advertising purposes. Beyond these mundane explanations for their existence, crop circles have generated interest among those who favor paranormal explanations for their origins. Among these are people who believe that UFOs are responsible for forming crop circles when they land, that crop circles are an effort on the part of a sentient planet Earth to communicate with humans, or the New Age belief that crop circles occur along energy flows between spiritually important sites. Regardless of the disparate views about their origin, crop circles have generated great interest. For example, a google search for the term "crop circle" yields over one million sites.

Goode argues that paranormal beliefs themselves are real, despite the fact that the basis for these beliefs themselves cannot be verified. He concludes that the persistence of paranormal beliefs represents a populist cultural countercurrent, which opposes the dominance of the scientific model in contemporary thinking. In other words, belief in a variety of paranormal beliefs indicates a subtle form of resistance to the cultural power of scientific rational thought. Furthermore, material involving paranormal beliefs seems to have enormous entertainment value; even people who doubt paranormal phenomena may find stories about them highly entertaining. Belief in the paranormal may also have a cognitive basis, as people tend to believe they see more uniformity/patterns in naturalistic phenomena than empirically exist. That is, humans may have a cognitive tendency to impose patterns where they don't already exist. Though some paranormal beliefs may directly oppose mainstream beliefs, many paranormal beliefs can exist as complementary to scientific beliefs. In fact, modern pluralistic societies are capable of tolerating contradictory beliefs, and on an individual basis, some persons are similarly capable of holding contradictory personal beliefs. As a rule, belief in the paranormal is deemed harmless and so are members of the related subcultures.

RESPONDING TO SUBCULTURES

Although persons at all ages can be involved in subcultures, youth subcultures seem to attract a lot of attention from those in authority positions, including police, teachers, and parents. In addition, youth subcultures are often discussed in the mass media, and youth styles are often co-opted by businesses wishing to turn a profit through the mass marketing of commodities such as music, jewelry, and clothing. Subcultural slang and gestures also often become absorbed by the mainstream; oppositional youth culture may in fact be marketed as cool. However, especially in the case of oppositional youth subcultures, many groups raise the ire of concerned citizens who worry that the persistence of subcultures spells an impending doom for conventional social values. This concern prompts an overarching question: How dangerous are subcultures?

Some subcultures, although they may exhibit beliefs and behaviors that differ from conventional values and lifestyles, pose little or no threat to the social order. Examples of relatively innocuous groups are discussed earlier in this chapter and include subcultures that comprise fans, people who believe in the paranormal, and youth groups assembled for purposes of identity seeking. Although such groups often raise the hackles of those interested in enforcing and maintaining traditional standards of propriety, such reactions may be disproportionately severe and incompatible with the very low threat level posed by such groups. In innocuous subcultures, opposition to the conventional is largely

Renegade Kids and Outlaw Youth

In their book *Renegade Kids, Suburban Outlaws,* Wayne Wooden and Randy Blazak differentiate between two types of youth subcultures, one benign and the other malignant. Renegade kids are those who belong to youth subcultures, mostly for the purposes of solving the problems of social life and identity seeking. These young people work to differentiate themselves socially from other cliques and therefore adopt distinctive fashion styles associated with subcultures. Renegade kids do not pose a serious threat to society and therefore should be treated as relatively innocuous. Examples include many punk rockers, skateboarders, mall rats, and other similar youth cliques. On the other hand, outlaw youth are those whose behaviors violate the law or other deeply held social standards and are dealt with seriously by community groups, school officials, and the justice system. The behaviors of outlaw youth have a disturbing quality, and therefore these groups and their actions are carefully monitored and opposed by mainstream social groups. Examples of outlaw youth include criminal youth gangs, tagger crews, skinheads, and satanic youth.

symbolic and unlikely to threaten the interests of the society at large. Many fringe subcultures also pose little threat to the society at large, particularly as these groups prefer to be left alone. Ethnic enclaves comprising individuals who steer clear of interactions with the mainstream (e.g., some immigrant groups, the Amish, and some religious groups) are similarly harmless.

On the other hand, there are subcultures that pose serious threats and are closely monitored. Some groups discussed in this chapter may pose real threats to the well-being of specific categories of individuals or may threaten important standards widely held by the society at large. Among these are white supremacists, some religious cults, and criminal gangs whose activities and beliefs can fundamentally menace deeply held social values and standards. Should the activities of these groups get out of control, they could indeed undermine social life writ large.

SUMMARY

The study of subcultures is an interesting part of the sociological study of deviancy and crime, because many subcultures are among the most innovative of social groups. Although the focus on subcultures in deviancy studies has emerged only in recent decades, we can expect that the field of subcultural studies will continue to flourish.

Further Reading

Brake, Michael. *Comparative Youth Culture*. Boston: Routledge, Keegan & Paul, 1985.

Goode, Erich. *Paranormal Beliefs: A Sociological Introduction*. Prospect Heights, Ill.: Waveland Press, 2000.

Haenfler, Ross. *Goths, Gamers, and Grrrls: Deviance and Youth Subcultures*. New York: Oxford University Press, 2009.

Hebdige, Dick. *Subculture: The Meaning of Style*. London: Methuen, 1979.

Wooden, Wayne, and Randy Blazak. *Renegade Kids, Suburban Outlaws: From Youth Culture to Delinquency*. Belmont, Calif.: Wadsworth, 2001.

Further Reading

CHAPTER 7

YOUTH CRIME AND DEVIANCE

Young people represent the literal and symbolic future of any social group. Thus, when they transgress social norms, particularly laws, the mainstream culture often feels threatened by a sense of impending social instability. Most youthful transgressions, however, are not that egregious. They are generally transgressions against social norms (not societal laws), a typical part of the maturation process and an expression of identity seeking. This means that the effective handling of youth deviance may be entirely different from handling norm violation by adults. Because youth are still maturing, responses to juvenile norm transgression tend to center on education and reintegration. This chapter begins with an overview of specific youth deviance and crime, how these differ from adult deviance and crime of similar types, and then examines the juvenile share of the overall crime problem, including offenses exclusively associated with youth.

JUVENILE DELINQUENCY AND ITS CAUSES

In American culture, there is the tendency to see youth as a group separate from the mainstream, one which has its own subcultural norms, fashions, and lingo. In the news media and popular discourse, we often hear of strange behaviors or shocking crimes committed by youth, and often these are taken as omens of youth's inability to live effectively within society. Youth are often identified as having strange styles, forms of interaction, or priorities. One contradiction is that some strange behaviors are attributed to all youth, whereas others are attributed to particular youth subcultures. For example, the horrific behavior of a small group of troubled youth who carry out school shootings has at times stimulated a wider discussion about youth in general as a social problem. This in turn leads to confusion in the public discourse regarding the status of youth, with some intimating that all youth are problematic, and others suggesting that only certain subsets of youth are problematic. While juveniles in general may demonstrate some aspects of a subculture that is distinct from the adult culture or subcultures, it is also true that these juveniles live with and are integrated within family units that are part of the society at large. Thus, it may be more appropriate to conceptualize youth as a group occupying a different stage of the life course from that occupied by adults. Thus, instead of viewing youth deviancy as generic, discerning students of deviancy might try differentiating between harmful youth groups and those who, though strange, are relatively benign.

Juvenile delinquency refers to violations of criminal law and other forms of antisocial behaviors committed by youthful offenders, typically those 17 years of age or younger. The causes of juvenile delinquency correspond closely with the causes of crime in general as discussed in Chapter 3 of this text. In most cases, transgressions against law result from a combination of the following factors: individual choice and the influence of structural factors, such as poverty or culture. But although juvenile delinquency is a product of individual choice and structural factors, it can also be attributed to the improper functioning of institutions of socialization. **Socialization** is a process through which individuals learn the beliefs and behaviors necessary for social life within a given group. It includes attaining fluency in the appropriate norms, social roles, and patterns of communication of that group. As the lessons are learned and absorbed, the socialization process becomes a mechanism through which social stability and conformity are accomplished. In modern societies, the socialization process takes place primarily within three institutions: family, school, and peer groups.

The family is arguably the most influential institution of socialization. Before reaching the age of 4 or 5, children tend to interact almost exclusively with family members. Until approximately age 12, the family continues to serve as the primary reference group after which children model their behaviors. Children learn values and behaviors through modeling the behaviors of older family members. One of the biggest risk factors associated with delinquency emerges when children learn antisocial norms and behaviors from family members. It is easy to see how being raised by criminal parents can be a primary risk for youth; however, many parents with mainstream values also raise children who engage in delinquent behaviors, and there are criminal parents who raise their children in a manner that inculcates mainstream values. Thus, the development of delinquent values is not something solely determined by environment. For this reason (among others), social scientists focus on risk factors which may increase the likelihood that a youth might become delinquent, but do so with the caveat that these risk factors do not deterministically cause delinquency.

Parenting style is one factor that can promote or deter youth delinquency. Parents who maintain high expectations for their children's behavior and who offer adequate support for their children to reach those expectations tend to raise well-adjusted children. Conversely, parents who maintain low expectations for their children's behavior and who do not support their children's endeavors are more likely to raise delinquent children. Also related to parenting style is the fact that children who are inadequately supervised are more likely to misbehave. The bonds formed (or not formed) between parents and children is also a significant aspect of socialization. Children who spend quality time with their parents and who have good relationships with them are less likely to engage in delinquent behaviors. Children who spend little quality time with their parents and have poor relationships with them are much more likely to engage in deviant or delinquent behaviors. It is worth pointing out that regardless of the amount of time children spend with parents, it is the quality of time spent together and the relationship that it shapes (for better or worse) that is most significant.

Family structure can also promote or deter delinquency. The presence of a biological mother in the home seems to trump all other factors relating to family structure. Indeed, social scientists have found that any family structure in which children are raised by their biological mother tends to be most effective in raising well-adjusted children. This is true whether the biological mother is a single parent living without a partner or whether she is living with a husband, the biological father, a step-father, or a boyfriend. Family structures without a biological mother seem to expose children to a comparatively higher risk of delinquent outcomes. This includes households with single fathers, with step-mothers, or with adoptive parents. Given these findings, public policy efforts to reduce delinquency often focus on keeping families together, to keep mothers with their children, and to teach parents effective child-rearing techniques.

Starting approximately at age 5, children spend a significant proportion of their time at school. Schools function as institutions of education where knowledge and skills are conveyed; however they also function as institutions of socialization where children and adolescents learn appropriate social behaviors and attitudes. Adequate performance in school is often closely related to appropriate social development in youth. Indeed, even with very young children, many schools use grading categories such as "plays well with others," which is analogous to evaluating whether or not a child behaves appropriately in social situations. As children age, they are no longer graded according to their social skills, but are instead graded for their performance in academic subjects.

Adequate performance in school is often interpreted as a proxy for normative behavior, and often social scientists view poor educational achievement as analogous to delinquency. In other words, those youth who do well in school are generally seen as better acclimated to social life, while those who perform poorly are at higher risk for delinquency. Children who have positive attitudes toward school are more likely to perform well in school, and vice versa. Simply put, if students believe that they can achieve good marks through concentrating on their work and studying harder, they often perform better. In contrast, students who believe that their academic success lies in areas outside their control (e.g., teacher subjectivity or favoritism) tend to demonstrate lower performance in school.

Because academic success is such an important factor for normative development, the number of young people who are apathetic about school is of great concern to American society at large. Disengaged students take little interest in their studies; moreover, they do not believe that education will enhance their future prospects, a condition that is associated with delinquency. Critics of the educational system point out that student engagement is not entirely the responsibility of students themselves, citing other factors that affect school engagement. One example is adequate family support for children; another is support for teachers from parents and school administrators. Indeed, many critics argue that the loss of teacher authority may be the big-

Apathetic student in class. Disengagement from school may put some students at risk for developing delinquent behavioral patterns. *(Shutterstock)*

Youth Gangs

A gang is a subcultural group that exists primarily for criminal purposes, and youth gangs are a subset of this category. Traditionally, youth gangs have consisted of members drawn from poverty-stricken areas in cities. Banding together for economic and social advancement through criminal enterprise, they formed "street gangs," a term often used interchangeably with "youth gangs." Youth gangs are considered subcultures because they utilize idiosyncratic signs (e.g., fashion signs, hand signals, tattoos, or argot) as communicative devices, and because they govern their behaviors according to countercultural norms. For example, youth gangs positively sanction the use of violence and profit seeking through criminal activities, such as drug dealing or extortion. Among subcultures, youth gangs generate a high level of social concern, as youth involved in gangs are highly likely to become career criminals as adults.

gest problem associated with poor behavior and poor academic performance in our nation's schools.

Starting at approximately age 12, and continuing through adolescence, youth most strongly model their behavior after the behavior(s) of their peers. Adolescents often engage in what is known as **groupthink**, which means that individual members of a group follow along with the general sentiment of the group, without consideration for their own preferences. The peer group with which a young person associates (and identifies) has a strong influence on his or her behavior and attitudes toward social life. Youth who associate with delinquent peers are at highest risk of delinquency themselves because they are socialized to adopt the deviant behaviors and attitudes of the group.

JUVENILE DELINQUENCY AS A SUBSET OF CRIME

As a subset of the UCR data collected by the FBI (discussed in Chapter 2 of this text), the Office of Juvenile Justice and Delinquency Prevention (OJJDP) tracks the nature and ratio of crimes committed by offenders under the age of 18. According to the OJJDP, in 2008 there were 2.11 million arrests of juveniles, and crimes committed by juveniles accounted for about 12 percent of the total violent crime problem and about 18 percent of the total property crime problem. Of the 2.11 million juvenile arrests in 2008, 30 percent were girls.

The UCR data indicate that trends in juvenile arrests strongly mirror the trends observed in adult offenses, both in violent crimes and property crimes (see Chapter 2). Figure 7.1 illustrates trends in juvenile arrests for the time period between 1980 and 2008. As the figure shows, arrests for youth violent offenses increased from the mid-1980s to the mid-1990s. Similar to adult violent

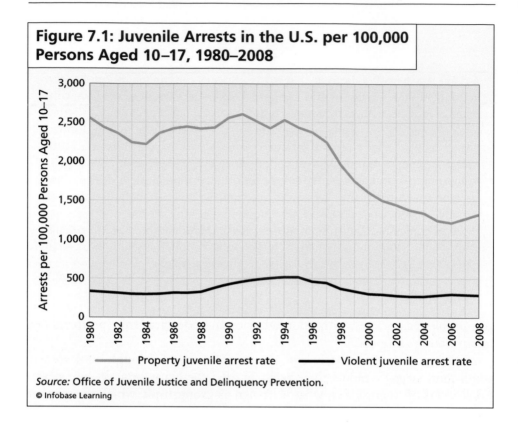

Figure 7.1: Juvenile Arrests in the U.S. per 100,000 Persons Aged 10–17, 1980–2008

Property juvenile arrest rate   Violent juvenile arrest rate

Source: Office of Juvenile Justice and Delinquency Prevention.
© Infobase Learning

offenses, youth violence seems to have peaked in the mid-1990s (specifically 1994), after which time youth violent offenses declined below rates observed in the 1980s. Generally, the rate of youth violence at present is low even though some high-profile cases seem to be driving a perception that youth violence is intensifying.

Also reflecting adult trends, youth property arrests have occurred at relatively high levels throughout the 1980s and early 1990s. In 1994, youth property offenses began a consistent decline until reaching the relatively low levels observed since the mid- to late-2000s. As is the case with adult levels of property crime, we are living in a period in which youth property offenses are considered relatively low.

Rates of juvenile offense vary along gender and racial lines. Typically, juvenile delinquency has been a social problem associated with boys, although in recent years the proportion of girls arrested for youth crime has increased. This increasing gender equality between boys and girls has been a cause of concern, as females were previously seen as less likely to engage in delinquency. (Note that some scholars see this as a sign that gender inequality is decreasing.) Vio-

Diversion Programs

The juvenile justice system employs a number of diversionary programs, which are programs that allow an offender to complete a punishment or treatment outside of juvenile court and thereby avoid a juvenile record. Diversion programs are widely used because typical adjudication and detention of youth offenders is considered to have a negative effect because it labels youthful offenders, more or less permanently. Diversion may involve education programs geared to preventing reoffending, restitution or mediation between offender and victim, community service, or injunctions to avoid places and persons deemed to be problematic. Within the juvenile justice system, diversionary programs are most widely utilized for first-time offenders, status offenders (i.e., those who engage in activities prohibited for minors but legal for adults), and youth with substance abuse and/or mental health issues.

lent offenses are still more strongly male-oriented, while girls are increasingly responsible for a share of property offenses. Although the rate of offense indicated in the UCR data shows an overall decline in juvenile offense, the rate of offense for adolescent females has declined less rapidly than it has for adolescent males, a trend which suggests cause for future concern. On the other hand, the rate of offense for black youth has declined more rapidly than the rate of offense for white youth. Although black youths continue to be overrepresented relative to the size of the black youth population, if current rates of offense continue, the trends will erase the racial differences in offence previously observed between white and black youth. This is a cause for optimism, as the racial barriers to delinquency prevention may be less severe in the current cultural climate than in past decades.

Aside from violent and property offenses (which are considered juvenile offenses only if they are committed by persons under the age of 18), there are a variety of other offenses exclusively associated with juveniles. Known as **status offenses**, these refer to behaviors that are prohibited for minors, but which adults can

Teenager attempts to hide his status offense from his mother. *(Shutterstock)*

lawfully undertake. Status offenses are quasi-criminal offenses that youth are prohibited from engaging in, simply because of their age. Examples include consumption of tobacco and alcohol, truancy, curfew violations, and running away from home. Youth under the age of 18 are prohibited from using tobacco, and those under the age of 21 are prohibited from consuming alcohol. By law, children are compelled to attend school and, in many municipalities, may be prohibited from being outside the home without a guardian past a set curfew time. Finally, youth are prohibited from running away from home. Figure 7.2 illustrates trends in some forms of status offenses, over the past three decades. Although the patterns of youth offenses in both violent and property crimes peaked in the mid-1990s and then declined sharply to their present levels, the trends in status offenses tell a more confusing story. Although the three varieties of status offenses that are presented in the figure are now at their lowest levels in three decades, the periods of changing violations do not seem to follow the same patterns as those for violent and property offenses. Social scientists suspect that status offenses may be separate phenomena within the juvenile delinquency problem and that theories explaining violent and property offenses cannot be applied to status offenses.

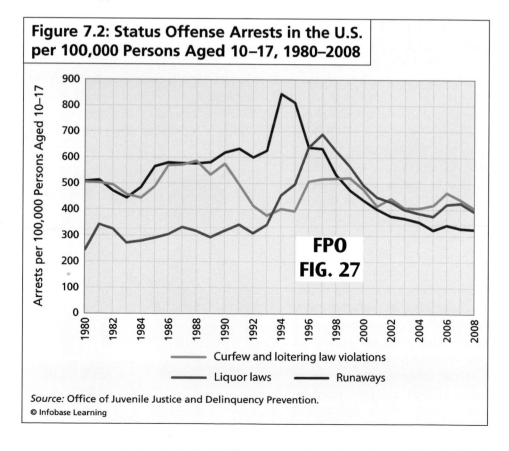

Figure 7.2: Status Offense Arrests in the U.S. per 100,000 Persons Aged 10–17, 1980–2008

FPO
FIG. 27

Curfew and loitering law violations

Liquor laws   Runaways

Source: Office of Juvenile Justice and Delinquency Prevention.
© Infobase Learning

Entering Delinquency

Some adolescents are described as **at-risk youth** if their behaviors or environments make them more likely to become delinquent. The assumption is that many youth face social crises and even though they may not themselves yet demonstrate delinquent behaviors, exposure to school violence, family violence/neglect, substance use/abuse, violent media, and **criminogenic** environments (e.g., living in gang neighborhoods) may put them at high risk of becoming delinquent. Various noncriminal activities may also be associated with being at-risk, and the following behaviors may reveal troubled adolescents: sexual promiscuity, teen pregnancy, mental/emotional disorders, eating disorders, and suicide behaviors. Some of the youth who display these behavioral characteristics may run away from home, ultimately ending up living on the streets or in juvenile detention. At-risk youth can demonstrate a variety of problem behaviors, which as a whole are considered **problem behavior syndrome** (PBS), which refers to a combination of antisocial behaviors or qualities that may make the youth more likely to engage in delinquency. These include factors on the social level (e.g., family dysfunction, poor academic performance, and misbehavior at school); the personal level (e.g., substance use, suicide, sexual promiscuity, premature parenthood, mental illnesses, and eating disorders); and the environmental level (e.g., living in a disorganized neighborhood/high-crime area and living in poverty).

Sociologist Rolf Loeber suggested that youth can follow one or more pathways toward delinquency, and that the behaviors along these pathways should be considered seriously because they may escalate into more severe behaviors:

- The **authority conflict pathway** begins at an early age (typically prior to age 12), when a child responds to authority with defiance or becomes stubborn. Children who insist on having things their own way and who are disobedient may eventually engage in authority evasion behaviors, which include staying out late, skipping school, and running away from home.
- The **covert pathway** typically begins at age 12 or later and involves concealed deviant behavior (such as lying or shoplifting) that can escalate into more serious forms of delinquency such as joyriding, larceny, burglary, fraud, vandalism, or arson.
- The **overt pathway** typically begins at age 12 or later, and involves belligerent acts (e.g., being a nuisance and bullying), which can lead to more serious forms of violence (such as gang involvement, fighting, and robbery).

Some delinquents might specialize in a small number of offenses, and therefore may have their behaviors limited to a single pathway, although other

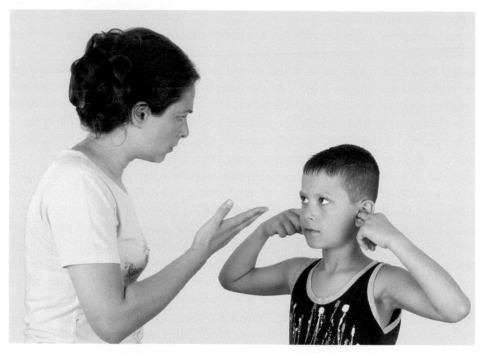

The authority conflict pathway begins when a child becomes stubborn and defiant when confronted by authority. *(Shutterstock)*

offenders are more eclectic in the choices of misbehavior. Typically, the age of onset for delinquent behavior is considered an important factor, with youth whose onset of delinquency comes earlier being considered at higher risk for continued criminal involvement. Although common logic suggests that youth who are aggressive and lack respect for others' property are more likely to become adults who act aggressively and lack respect for others' property, this is rarely the case. Perhaps counterintuitively, criminologists have consistently observed that although a large proportion of youth engage in some form of delinquency, only a small percentage of delinquent youth go on to become career criminals. Most youthful offenders engage in more-or-less typical teenage misbehavior, limiting deviant and even criminal acts to their adolescent years. On the other hand, a small number of youthful offenders begin their criminal careers during adolescence and continue those behaviors in adulthood. Research findings that most delinquent youth desist in such behaviors before reaching adulthood has been crucial in validating the juvenile justice system, which is based on the assumption that youth should not be permanently labeled or unduly punished for youthful misdeeds.

THE JUVENILE JUSTICE SYSTEM

Youth violation of criminal law has been of particular societal concern in the last century and has resulted in a parallel system of social response. It may come as a surprise that prior to the 20th century the life stage of adolescence (specifically, the stage of the life course falling between childhood and adulthood) did not exist as a biological and social category. In earlier times, children reached puberty later, often as late as 18 for boys and 16 to 17 for girls. This age range roughly corresponds with the legal age of majority still observed in many countries today. Currently, the onset of puberty comes much earlier, typically at age 12 or even sooner, and this has resulted in the conceptualization of adolescence as a stage in social development—one which pertains to the segment of the population that has achieved physical maturity but has not yet developed psychological maturity.

The life stage of adolescence emerged as a social construct to deal with social challenges arising from a somewhat novel stage in the life course, and this broad shift necessitated a new construct on how adolescents should be treated when they violated legal standards. Prior to the 19th century, youth criminals and adult criminals were subject to the same legal procedures and punishments. It was in the mid-19th century that social reformers began to argue that youthful offenders should be treated differently. Important in the development of this distinction was the idea that youthful offenders were still maturing and that their behaviors could be redirected in ways that could produce well-integrated, productive adults. In contrast, adult offenders were viewed as being relatively incorrigible and therefore incapable of reform. In addition, it was considered detrimental to young offenders to be housed in the same penal facilities as adult

Juvenile Waiver to Adult Court

Each year in the United States, about 8,000 youth under age 18 are transferred from juvenile court to adult court, where they are tried and sentenced as adults. Many of these youth may face extended prison sentences, and until recently, they could even be executed for extremely serious offenses. This practice reflects the public sentiment that the justice system should "get tough" on the worst offenders, regardless of their age. In 44 U.S. states, youthful offenders who commit extremely violent crimes (such as murder and some gang-related offenses) can be legally treated the same as adult offenders. Many of these states, however, maintain separate correctional facilities for juveniles convicted as adults. In most of these states, the minimum age for transferring youth offenders to adult court is 16 or 17; in some states, it can be as young as 13 or 14.

offenders, because the proximity to adult offenders would likely lead them to full socialization into criminal groups. Thus, a parallel **juvenile justice system** first emerged in the mid-19th century, one which aimed to protect youthful offenders from adult offenders and the criminal courts and, at the same time, aimed to reform youthful offenders so that they would become productive members of society. The juvenile justice system included juvenile courts and juvenile detention centers. At the same time, it created a new category of offender, which differentiate between youth offenders and adult offenders: Youth offenders were assigned the new designation of "juvenile delinquents" whereas adult offenders continued to be labeled as criminals.

The juvenile justice system has an explicitly rehabilitative philosophy because it operates under the assumption that youth offenders can be reformed and that there is a high probability that they can be steered into well-adjusted adult lives. Reflecting and supporting this philosophy is a separate vocabulary, which the juvenile justice system employs in an effort to avoid negatively labeling young offenders. For example, youth are "adjudicated" whereas adults are "tried" in court; youth are determined to be "delinquent" or "not delinquent" whereas adults are found "guilty" or "not guilty." The punishment phase of the

The Columbine High School Shootings

In the last decade and a half, horrific shootings at schools have occurred in the United States as well as in other countries. In the United States, the 1999 shootings at Columbine High School in Colorado stands out as the most infamous high school shooting. Two students failed in their attempt to blow up the school, but then went on a shooting spree during which they killed 12 other students, one teacher, and themselves. What many people found particularly shocking about the event was the nihilism expressed by the offenders who seemed to enjoy stalking and killing their classmates. Columbine sparked a national debate on the status of youth, prompting a hard look at American youth and strong concerns that youth was in crisis. The term "Columbine" became synonymous with a complex set of fears and anxieties surrounding youth violence and youth-related social problems in America. Although Columbine-type attacks are extremely rare, their consequences are grave. One of the consequences is that Columbine and subsequent school attacks have become almost emblematic, painting all youth offenses and all youthful offenders with the same brush. As a result of Columbine, a number of schools increased security measures, introducing surveillance cameras, metal detectors, and police officers patrolling corridors and cafeterias. Critics of such security measures point out that creating an airport-like security environment in schools is antithetical to the institutional goals of nurturing and educating children.

youth and adult systems also differs. Adult criminals are sentenced to serve prison sentences; youthful offenders are likely to be mandated to pursue academic instruction, vocational education, or instruction in life skills such as anger management, substance abuse treatment, and conflict resolution. Some juvenile detention centers focus on behavioral modification, intended to help youth offenders learn pro-social behaviors and attitudes.

The overarching goal of the juvenile justice system is to maintain a separate justice process for youth, one which offers them the maximum chance of amending their behaviors and returning to normal life. When a youthful offender turns 18, the juvenile record is sealed or expunged. This allows the youth to start adult life without a record of legal transgression and without the stigma of delinquency.

Because the juvenile justice system is concerned with the effective development of youth in its charge, it is often seen as filling a quasi-parenting role. In legal terms, the state operates in **parens patriae** (a Latin phrase meaning "parent of the nation"), which means that the state takes responsibility for those children who lack proper parents to raise them, whether because the parents are absent or because the parents (though present) are so poor at parenting that the child has been negatively influenced and inappropriately socialized. The state then takes a role in the positive socialization of youth, and in the case of the juvenile justice system, intervenes when children violate legal standards and are at risk of gravitating into lives of crime. Thus, the juvenile justice system operates as an institution of socialization when other, traditional institutions (including family, schools, and peer groups) do not function effectively.

SUMMARY
Youth crimes concern citizens and sociologists alike, partly because youth become adults and behavior exhibited in youth may continue into adulthood and escalate throughout the life course. A greater concern is that juvenile delinquency may reflect the ineffective functioning of the institutions that typically accomplish socialization of youth: the family, schools, and peer groups. While the phenomena of youth crime and deviance share similarities with adult crimes and deviance, there are crucial differences in patterns, causes, and motivations. Above all, youth are treated differently (and are subject to a separate juvenile justice system) because they are at a different stage in the life course.

Further Reading

Aarons, John, Lisa Smith, and Linda Wagner. *Dispatches from Juvenile Hall: Fixing a Failing System.* New York: Penguin, 2009.
Chesney-Lind, Meda. *Girls, Delinquency, and Juvenile Justice.* New York: Wadsworth, 2003.

Haenflaer, Ross. *Goths, Gamers, & Grrrls.* New York: Oxford University Press, 2010.

Hume, Edward. *No Matter How Loud I Shout: A Year in the Life of Juvenile Court.* New York: Simon & Schuster, 1997.

Office of Juvenile Justice and Delinquency Prevention 2011. Statistical briefing book. Available at http://www.ojjdp.gov/ojstatbb/.

Office of Juvenile Justice and Delinquency Prevention. Juvenile arrests 2008. Available at http://www.ncjrs.gov/pdffiles1/ojjdp/228479.pdf.

Reich, Adam. *Hidden Truth: Young Men Navigating Lives In and Out of Juvenile Prison.* Berkeley, Calif.: Univ. of California Press, 2010.

Short, James F., and Lorine A. Hughes. *Juvenile Delinquency and Delinquents: The Nexus of Social Change.* Upper Saddle River, N.J.: Pearson Prentice Hall, 2008.

CHAPTER 8

POSITIVE SOCIAL ASPECTS OF CRIME AND DEVIANCY

Much of the discussion related to crime and deviance tends to focus on negative aspects of these behaviors, often with good cause. However, any text on the sociology of criminality and deviancy would be incomplete without some discussion of the positive aspects of these social phenomena. Put simply, sometimes people break laws that are unfair and ought to be broken, and the transgression of these legal codes, in turn, may lead to needed revisions in the law. Indeed, some people are deviant because they are unusually good. In addition, social environments sometimes breed mediocrity, and those who are better than average (and thus positively deviant) may experience social condemnation in a similar way as those who are deviant in the negative sense. As this chapter points out, deviance and crime have some latent positive qualities for the social world, which are often overlooked. More concretely, a good measure of positive social change comes when folks violate normative standards, especially if their transgressions result in revisions of social norms to promote higher moral or ethical standards. Thus, this chapter explores some of the positive aspects of deviancy, specifically deviance as a means of innovation, as an avenue for creating positive social change, or as a mechanism through which persons can differentiate themselves from others in positive ways.

POSITIVE ASPECTS OF NORM TRANSGRESSION
Many groups whose members violate folkway-type norms are relatively innocuous, including dorks, nerds, and geeks. Using a harm-based standard, there is no

verifiable injury that comes to the social world when nerds behave awkwardly in social situations. In comparison, we also see that violent crimes such as murder and rape definitely cause harm not only to the victims directly affected, but also to society as a whole because members of that society lose the sense of security and peace. However, what happens when, using a *harm-based standard*, some transgressive behaviors are actually beneficial to those affected by them and to society at large? Such cases force us to move beyond typical thinking about crime and deviance as negative aspects of society and consider that a subset of crime and deviance can potentially generate social benefits.

When one pays close attention to deviant behavior, one often finds that human beings can be extremely creative and innovative. American culture, in fact, generally rewards innovation and discovery, even though most Americans may feel ambivalent when those innovations violate moral or legal standards. The bottom line remains that innovation is often an engine of social change, and some beliefs or practices that are considered strange or offensive at one time may with time become accepted or even encouraged.

According to the sociologist Robert K. Merton, social norms are defined in relationship to the cultural goals and to the accepted means of achieving those goals. Those who socially conform tend to abide by both the goals and the means. For example, American culture values financial success (a cultural goal) through hard work and self-discipline (the accepted means). In contrast, **innovators** accept the goals of the wider culture while rejecting the legitimate means for achieving those goals. Innovators develop their own methods for achieving their goals, in novel ways that are sometimes rejected by the society. However, it is often the case that new modes of behavior are eventually recognized as valuable contributions to the social world. For example, many computer hackers find useful employment in computer security firms, and former thieves are sometimes hired as security consultants to help protect corporations against theft. Thus, behaviors rejected by the mainstream culture as deviant and/or criminal can become innovative methods for making a positive contribution to society.

Another category of deviants who might occasionally be socially useful are **rebels**. In rejecting conventional goals and avenues for success, rebels create their own goals and their own methods of achieving those goals. Rebel groups often display congruence between their goals and means, although both differ from those of the mainstream society. Many subcultural groups are populated by rebels and follow their own set of values, working in novel ways to achieve those values. Some positively contribute to the society at large because their values instigate behaviors that make them constructively involved in the broader society. For example, religious groups whose values are communal and service oriented may shun typical employment in favor of direct service to those in need. Although they may reject both the typical American value of material success and the method of work-for-pay to achieve success, they may nonetheless be of valuable service to the needy and the wider society in general.

Civil Disobedience
In cases where laws are repressive of human or civil rights, many individuals engage in **civil disobedience**, which is the refusal to obey certain laws, rules, or government mandates, typically (though not always) in the form of nonviolent demonstrations or resistance. The term civil disobedience is attributed to the 19th century American writer and activist Henry David Thoreau, though the practice has been used around the world for centuries.

Acts of civil disobedience violate laws or social policies in order to communicate messages that the laws or the policies they contest are unjust. In most cases, this occurs when government actions or laws conflict with deeply held moral or ethical standards. For example, in the antebellum South, those who opposed the enslavement of African Americans became active in the Underground Railroad to help escaped slaves move to the Northern states or Canada. In the mid-20th century Mahatma Gandhi and his followers used nonviolent resistance to depose the British colonial government in India. In the 1960s, the civil rights movement used boycotts and peaceful marches to achieve its goal of establishing civil rights for all Americans, regardless of race. Those active in the civil rights movement were protesting racial segregation and other forms of racial bias.

Henry David Thoreau's "Civil Disobedience"

Originally titled "Resistance to Civil Government," Henry David Thoreau's essay "Civil Disobedience" is a classic in political activism and social responsibility. In the essay, Thoreau argues that citizens should not tolerate immoral or unjust behaviors on the part of governments and are morally obligated to protest and violate unjust laws and public policies, rather than allowing their moral sensibilities to degenerate. Thoreau was motivated to write the essay because of two things he found repugnant: the institution of slavery in Southern states and the Mexican-American War, which Thoreau opposed as a pacifist.

Thoreau felt that most forms of government were at best corrupt and at worst unjust. Thus, he felt it was the duty of honest citizens to protest government misdeeds by actively breaking unjust laws rather than passively waiting to vote for more just policies. Thoreau himself was briefly imprisoned for failing to pay a tax that he felt was unjust. Thoreau's ideas in "Civil Disobedience" have influenced some of history's best-known campaigners for social justice, including Mahatma Gandhi and Martin Luther King, Jr.

Civil disobedience manifests itself in many forms. Some definitions of civil disobedience stipulate nonviolence, rejecting violent protest. Other definitions include violent protests as components of civil disobedience, although Thoreau originally intended the term to refer to nonviolent protests. Some forms of civil disobedience are revolutionary in that they are intended to overthrow an exist-

The March on Washington in 1963 was a pivotal moment during the civil rights movement. *(Library of Congress)*

Rosa Parks

Some acts of civil disobedience start with individuals engaging in solitary and relatively modest actions that violate oppressive laws or policies. One woman whose action sparked a flood of much greater responses was Rosa Parks, an African American civil rights activist, often considered the First Lady of Civil Rights. Ms. Parks lived in Montgomery, Alabama, which operated racially segregated public buses in which front seats were reserved for whites whereas blacks were forced to sit in the back. On December 1, 1955, Rosa Parks refused to obey the bus driver's order to vacate her seat for a white passenger. She was arrested and charged with violating municipal segregation laws. Her simple act of civil disobedience is cited as the spark that ignited the Montgomery Bus Boycott, when African American passengers refused to ride the Montgomery public transport system. The Montgomery Bus Boycott became the first in a series of protests comprising the American civil rights movement.

ing government that is deemed to be unjust; nonrevolutionary forms intend to amend existing laws and policies that are deemed unjust. At times civil disobedience is carried out as part of collective action that may be associated with a subculture (as in the case of political movements); in other cases civil disobedience may be solitary acts where a lone person refuses to comply with authorities.

In terms of the specific actions undertaken, civil disobedience can vary widely. For example, some acts may be relatively benign, posing little more than a nuisance (e.g., trespassing on the site of a factory to protest pollution or at military facility to protest war). Some acts of civil disobedience may be symbolic gestures. Examples might include criticizing public figures, violating decency standards (in the cases of those who advocate nudism), or defacing official Websites. Other forms of disobedience may create greater problems for authorities and include, for example, boycotting government run services, refusing to pay taxes, avoiding military service, and staging sit-ins which disrupt the functioning of public and private services.

Whereas some individuals practicing civil disobedience resist law enforcement figures and agencies, others peacefully cooperate with them by allowing themselves to be arrested and even imprisoned. In the latter cases, protesters often hope to overwhelm the capacity of law enforcement to arrest and process the sheer volume of offenders taken into custody. The legal processing of those who engage in civil disobedience (particularly in its innocuous and nonviolent forms) varies greatly. Legal prosecutors and juries often have difficulty attributing *mens rea* (i.e., malicious intent) to acts of civil disobedience, and therefore many nonviolent protests may go unpunished by the criminal justice system.

Members of the immigration reform movement engage in acts of civil disobedience by staging a sit-in. *(Wikipedia)*

At its heart, the purpose and role of civil disobedience is to point out ethical or moral injustices within public policies and legal practices, even when the social environment of the times condones and supports such policies and practices. When civil disobedience is successful, it may bring about positive and sweeping social change. Indeed, many of the brightest moments in American history were prompted by activists engaging in activities that were considered deviant and criminal. The civil rights movement and the legal and social changes it spearheaded is a classic example.

What complicates the issue of civil disobedience is that we often observe a lack of widespread consensus about what constitutes positive social change. It is, for example, often possible to observe civil disobedience activists supporting or rejecting the same policy, sometimes at the same time and in the same location. Take, for example, efforts by anti-abortion groups and pro-choice groups to influence public and legal opinions on the issue of abortion rights.

GOOD BEHAVIOR AS DEVIANT

In American society, competition and personal gain operate as strong values influencing social behaviors. Because people are supposed to look out for themselves, it might be considered odd to manifest a high level of concern for the

Paolo Freire and "Conscientization"

Brazilian critical education theorist Paolo Freire coined the Portuguese-language term *conscientização*, which translates as "critical consciousness" or "consciousness raising," a phenomenon that encourages those studying society to pair in-depth knowledge of social dynamics with activist work to oppose unfair aspects of society. Commonly termed "conscientization" in English, the process particularly involves raising the awareness of oppressed persons about their oppression and then asking them to refute those aspects of society that contribute to the oppression. For example, in the United States the poor may feel that they are inferior and therefore that they deserve impoverishment as a reflection of their own shortcomings. Because educational access for the poor is often limited to substandard schools, the poor presumably have little or no ability to refute the structural aspects of their own repression. Conscientization among the poor would advocate increasing critical education for this group so that members of the group can refute the self-defeating aspects of poverty and thereby improve not only their own lot but bring about positive social change that improves the lots of others as well.

welfare of others. We observe that some individuals or groups more strongly establish the norm of altruism, and these groups may be perceived as strange or even suspect. Some individuals and groups make it a point routinely to do good deeds for others, often expecting nothing in return. And although it may contradict common sense, good deeds may sometimes be interpreted as deviant.

A pessimist might say that "no good deed goes unpunished," and life teaches us that this proverb is not as far-fetched as it might seem. In real-life social interactions, many do-gooders get criticized for their well-intentioned behaviors. Sometimes because the good intent backfires and sometimes because the behavior is viewed with cynicism (even by the person it benefits). **Altruism**, defined as the selfless concern for the well-being of others, has long been the overt standard in many religious traditions. However, the practical standard of social behavior often falls far short of the lofty goal of true altruism. Most often people treat others according to how they view those others and whether they deem those others deserving. Moreover, as humans are far from perfect, our altruistic deeds may not always be what the object of our altruism needs or wants.

A recent and relatively widespread cultural manifestation of altruism is performing **random acts of kindness** (also known as RAKs), which are selfless acts performed with no expectation of reciprocity. The term is said to have been coined by peace activist Anne Herbert in the early 1980s, when she wrote the following motto on a Sausalito, California restaurant placemat: "Practice

Boy Scouts and Good Deeds

The Boy Scouts have a well-known tradition of encouraging members to do one good deed per day. According to James E. West, the first Executive Director of the Boy Scouts, "Selfishness is almost a universal evil. Certainly it is overcome by the Scout Program, which is based upon the development of service for others, and the Daily Good Turn [i.e., Good Deed] is an important factor in the development of a habit of service and attitude of mind which offset a tendency to selfishness."

West felt that performing a single good deed in service to another once per day would build a habit of altruism, which would benefit not only those undertaking the good deed but also the world at large. Therefore, Boy Scouts were instructed to do one selfless deed per day, whether that good deed benefited other individuals, the community, the nation, animals, or nature. Although the clichéd good deed performed by a Boy Scout is to help an elderly woman cross a street, Boy Scout members have performed many millions of good deeds over the years.

random acts of kindness and senseless acts of beauty." Since then, the term and its underlying idea have been used in popular culture in a variety of places, including movies and books.

One of the most famous RAKs mentioned in human literature comes from the Parable of the Good Samaritan, which appears in the Christian Gospel of

Pay It Forward

The 2000 movie *Pay It Forward*, based on a book of the same name by Catherine Ryan Hyde, provides a good example of random acts of kindness in popular culture. The main character in the story is Trevor, an 11-year-old middle school student who is presented by his social studies teacher with an assignment to effect positive change in the world. Trevor devises a plan called "paying it forward" in which he performs three acts of kindness for three people he encounters. He then instructs each of them not to reciprocate directly but to "pay it forward" by doing three acts of kindness for three other people, whom they should also instruct to pay it forward. The story is a dramatic example of how kindness can be transformative, not only for those who receive but for those who give. The idea of "paying it forward" has reached beyond the influence of the movie itself, as many individuals have adopted the idea as a way of bringing about positive social change. For more information, start at the Website of the Pay It Forward Foundation: <www.payitforward.org>.

Modern-day Good Samaritans, members of AmeriCorps build a house with Habitat for Humanity. *(Wikipedia)*

Luke. In the story, a traveler is robbed, severely beaten, and left for dead along a road. Many persons pass by the wounded traveler, preferring not to get involved. Finally, a man goes out of his way to help the injured man. In the story, the man who helps the injured man is from Samaria—hence the Good Samaritan. In popular discourse, a "Good Samaritan" is a person who goes out of his or her way to help others, expecting no reward.

The idea of doing good deeds without expecting return is extremely old in human history. In Indian religious traditions, for example, the concept of karma attributes an indirect cause and effect to good and/or bad deeds. Basically, karma means that a person who does good deeds can expect good things to come into his or her life. Conversely, karma also says that bad deeds tend to flow back to a person who has committed bad deeds.

Both karma and RAK are based on the controversial idea of indirect reciprocity. Reciprocity is a relation of mutual exchange, and in informal relations reciprocity serves as a basis of human interactions. In its most basic form, reciprocity means that a person offering something of value can expect to receive something of value in return. The most common form of reciprocity is direct reciprocity, where a person receives something of value directly in return for something offered. However, karma and RAK operate under the principle of indirect reciprocity, where a person does not expect something in return, or if a person does expect reciprocity, it should be undertaken indirectly. "Paying it forward" is a good example of indirect reciprocity, where good deeds are intended to be repaid not to the person offering them but to others who are in need. Other conceptions of indirect reciprocity include the idea that good deeds will be rewarded in the afterlife and the idea that good deeds contribute to the general goodness in the world.

What is perhaps so controversial about indirect reciprocity is that some individuals may have difficulty reconciling a truly altruistic act, as it is generally assumed that people follow economic rationality even if they are genuinely engaged in selfless acts. Therefore, when offered a gift or a kind act, many recipients suspect an ulterior motive. You might try this yourself by offering some random acts of kindness. For suggestions, visit the Web site for the Random Acts of Kindness Foundation <www.randomactsofkindness.org>, and check under the "Kindness Ideas" link.

Often, those who offer kindness are met with suspicion or even hostility, as if they harbor hidden agendas. Experiencing this interesting sort of response can be helpful in understanding how the social system potentially suppresses positive behaviors using the same mechanisms that are used to suppress negative behaviors. Of course, some people do con others by seeming to approach them with kindness, while harboring covert intentions to manipulate their good will, so it is useful to have a healthy level of skepticism. All things consid-

My Name Is Earl

The TV comedy sitcom *My Name is Earl* was created by Greg Garcia and originally ran from 2005 to 2009 on the NBC television network. The series centers on the antics of the title character, Earl Hickey (played by Jason Lee), and his efforts to earn good karma by performing good deeds. In the first episode, Earl is a small-time criminal whose winning instant lottery ticket is lost when he is hit by a car. While recovering in a hospital, Earl sees a TV program about karma, and he is inspired by the idea of karmic retribution. In reflecting on his life, Earl discovers that he has done a number of bad deeds, which he comes to believe explain why bad things happen to him. With this thought, Earl resolves to make a list of all the bad things he has ever done and then to make amends for his wrongdoings. After he makes amends for his first bad deed, Earl finds his lost lottery ticket, a sign which he interprets as a karmic reward. For the remainder of the four seasons that the series ran, each episode centered on Earl fixing the damage caused by his various bad deeds. The concept of the show is interesting because it involves karma (typically seen as a form of indirect reciprocity) in a direct form of reciprocity as Earl rights the various wrongs he caused others in the past.

ered, however, it can also be fruitful for scholars of crime and deviance to study some of the positive aspects of norm transgression, not only in cases which are intended to protest injustice, but also in cases where the intention is simply to do a good turn.

SUMMARY

The positive aspects of crime and deviance rarely get much attention. If anything, those breaking rules provide employment and challenges for those whose jobs are to enforce rules. But positive aspects of deviance exist and may be more widespread than most people might think. They range from acts of civil disobedience and other rule-breaking behaviors which lead to positive social change to good deeds and random acts of kindness "perpetrated" on total strangers or life-giving and life-affirming activities organized by altruistic institutions or organizations.

Further Reading

Boles, Nicole Bouchard. *How to Be an Everyday Philanthropist: 330 Ways to make a Difference in Your Home, Community, and World—at No Cost!* New York: Workman Publishing, 2009.

Hyde, Catherine Ryan. *Pay it Forward.* Reprint Edition. New York: Simon & Schuster, 2010.

Kinchloe, Joe L. *Critical Pedagogy Primer*, 2nd ed. New York: Peter Lang Publishing, 2008.

Leder, Mimi (director). *Pay It Forward.* 2000. DVD (123 minutes).

Pay It Forward Foundation. Home page. Available at http://www.payitforwardfoundation.org/.

Random Acts of Kindness Foundation. Random acts of kindness. Available at http://www.randomactsofkindness.org/.

Salzburg, Sharon. *The Force of Kindness: Change Your Life with Love and Compassion.* Boulder, CO: Sounds True, Inc. 2010.

Thoreau, Henry David. "Civil Disobedience." Available at http://www.gutenberg.org/ebooks/71, 1849.

Wolens, Doug (director). *Butterfly.* 2000. DVD (79 minutes).

CHAPTER 9

SOCIAL RESPONSES TO CRIME AND DEVIANCE

There has never been (and likely never will be) a society without some form of deviance, and it seems that deviant behavior must play an important social function, even if the immediate consequences of deviance are negative. As some sociologists point out, norm transgression plays an important part in the typical social mechanism. Without deviance, the norms themselves might remain hidden or unclear, especially in the case of folkway- and more-type norms which are often unspoken and unwritten. Deviance helps to define social norms, which though they may seem self-evident, may remain ambiguous in the absence of norm transgressing behaviors. The potential for this condition is particularly pronounced in modern, pluralistic societies where social standards vary widely and change rapidly. This concluding chapter explores these issues by examining norm transgression and its relationship to the enforcement of norms, social change, and the evolution of forms of deviance, as exemplified by criminal violations related to crimes of vice.

On mundane levels, many violations of social norms arouse control responses. However, if norms and their violation remain unclear without the presence of behavior that breaks the norms, how does a social group differentiate between appropriate and inappropriate behavior? From a subjective point of view, many private or unrecognized violations of norms occur. But as previously explained, if such violations go undetected, they cannot be identified as deviant. The deviant label can be applied only when and if an act or behavior is seen or recognized as something outside normative boundaries. Therefore, it is the control response itself that clarifies deviance, and the deviance that clarifies the norms. When deviant behavior stimulates a social control response, it mobilizes a group to define the normative standards for behavior. In extreme cases where people are outraged by extreme forms of norm transgression, deviant behavior can help to build social consensus about the moral foundations of society and increase social solidarity.

Social control in its various forms (e.g., internal vs. external; informal vs. formal) was first discussed in Chapter 1 of this text. Most control responses are mild or subtle, serving as gentle reminders that a norm has been transgressed. For example, a parent's correction of a child reminds the child of the boundaries of propriety, or a speeding ticket reminds a motorist that a speed limit exists and is enforced. Of course, social control responses can also be more severe. One of the most extreme forms of control response is known as **moral panic**, defined as an intensity of emotion and concern expressed by a social group that perceives a threat to its basic social order.

Folk Devils and Moral Panics by Stanley Cohen

Published in 1972, Cohen's classic work describes extreme responses to deviance seen to be threatening to the social order. Cohen states that a moral panic exists when a "condition, episode, person or group of persons emerges to become defined as a threat to societal values and interests." The persons or groups responsible for the behavior that instigates the panic are known as "folk devils," who often are vociferously persecuted. Folk devils are perceived to threaten the moral order of society to such an extent that the general social response is a panic. With this onset of panic, the moral sentiments of the group are reasserted and reaffirmed. Moral panics are perhaps the most extreme cases of social control responses, and they are characterized by heightened concern about deviant behaviors and great levels of hostility toward those violating the norms. They spark a large consensus about the need to combat the threat to social order, even though the perceived threat is by definition disproportionately higher than the verifiable threat that has actually been posed. Finally, responses to folk devils can be very volatile, easily erupting into violence, although also receding rapidly once public interest has moved to another topic. Historical examples of moral panics include the following episodes of American history and examples of American pop culture: witch trials, anti-Communist trials under McCarthyism, heightened concern about the ills associated with pop music (e.g., heavy metal music), role playing games (e.g., Dungeons and Dragons), and video games (e.g., Grand Theft Auto).

Criminal Justice

Beyond the relatively common, mild forms of social control and the rare extreme forms of social control, are numerous serious and systematic responses to transgressions of social norms. In modern societies, such systematic and measured responses are the purview of the **criminal justice system**, which is a formal network of social institutions charged with enforcement, adjudication, and punishment related to transgressions of law. The criminal justice system includes law enforcement, courts, and corrections; three institutions that work together in responding to crime.

Law Enforcement

Police are agents of the government who are charged with the legitimate duty to enforce laws, protect property, and maintain public order. Typically, police are afforded a monopoly on the legitimate use of force within their geographic boundaries, and police agencies utilize a hierarchical structure that resembles

Brooklyn professor testifies before the House Un-American Committee during the McCarthy era. (Library of Congress)

Railway station with a deteriorated facade. Such conditions may signal to criminals that the area is an easy mark. *(Wikipedia)*

a military chain of command. Police organizations have been a facet of modern societies for approximately two centuries, and over time the role of police has evolved. The traditional role of police was considered **crime control**, a role in which police were expected to prevent criminal acts and apprehend those who break the law. Certainly police agencies continue in their crime control efforts, but in recent decades many police agencies have increasingly engaged in community policing, that is, working to reduce crime by helping to maintain the public order.

In 1982, James Q. Wilson and George L. Kelling published an article called "Broken Windows," in which they argued that physical signs of disorder and deterioration (e.g., broken windows on buildings, burned out streetlights, and graffiti) sent a message to would-be criminal offenders that neighborhoods in which such conditions were evident were easy targets. As a response, many police agencies implemented efforts to work with communities to clean up signs of deterioration and thereby to help residents of crime-ridden communities send a message that crime would not be tolerated. This approach is known as the **fixing broken windows** approach to policing, and the focus of such efforts is to maintain the physical aspects of neighborhoods and increase monitoring of locations where crimes might take place. Given this dual role (crime control and fixing broken windows), contemporary police agencies are active in a wide variety of activities in which they work directly to combat crime and indirectly to help communities maintain a better sense of order. Indeed, the public order maintenance of policing has become an increasing aspect of these agencies' mandates.

Courts

When police do arrest someone for violating the law, the accused person is remanded to the custody of the **court**, which is the institution associated with the administration of justice according to the rule of law and according to legally sanctioned procedures. In a practical sense, courts ensure legal fairness and procedural integrity to determine the culpability of accused parties. In cases where a person is determined to be responsible for a violation of law, the courts also determine appropriate penalties, which most frequently consist of probation, fines, and/or imprisonment. The most common popular image of the court system is that of prosecution and defense attorneys engaging one another in an adversarial manner until a verdict is reached and justice is served. In reality, only a small proportion of legal cases ever reach court, and a large percentage of cases involve more expedient processes, which generally involve negotiations. For example, defendants can plea bargain, which means that they may agree to plead guilty to a lesser crime rather than the crime they were originally charged

Courtroom in Nelson, Nebraska. *(Wikipedia)*

Problem-Solving Courts

A relatively new development in the court system has been the emergence of problem-solving courts where key stakeholders in the justice system (e.g., the prosecution, the defense, social workers, and probation officers) cooperate to reach the best possible outcome of a case. Suppose, for instance, that a person addicted to drugs has been arrested and accused of a drug violation. Once it has been determined that the defendant has a drug addiction, the court might offer reduced jail time if the defendant agrees to participate in a drug treatment program. Such courts attempt to reduce the strain on the criminal justice system, and to correct the underlying problems in a given case. Problem-solving courts have been used for a variety of offenses, including many juvenile violations, drug violations, cases of domestic violence, and violations caused by mental illness.

with in exchange for a reduced sentence or a lesser fine. In addition, a great number of cases are dismissed because the prosecution lacks sufficient evidence to prove a defendant's culpability.

Corrections

When an individual is found guilty for a violation of law, the **corrections** component of the criminal justice system becomes responsible for administration of punishment. Punishment comes in various forms, including imprisonment, probation, and rehabilitation. The most common form of punishment is probation, a specified period of time during which an offender is ordered to comply with specific restrictions set by the court. These restrictions can include any combination of the following: prohibited possession of firearms, avoiding alcohol and drugs, maintaining a job, living in a certain location, submitting to searches and/or drug tests, and wearing an electronic monitoring device. In addition, offenders on probation are required to report periodically to their probation officers, and they may be ordered to complete substance abuse treatment, mental health treatment, or community service.

In cases where an offense is more severe, an offender may be incarcerated in a jail or prison. Jails typically house prisoners serving sentences of less than six months; prisons house offenders serving sentences of more than six months. The philosophy of corrections fits on a continuum between the rehabilitative and the punitive. Some see the role of prisons as rehabilitative, with the objective of resocializing offenders so that they can rejoin society to become productive citizens after serving their time. Others see the role of prisons in a more punitive light, as a means of exacting punishment on offenders as retribution for violations of the law. Compared to other countries, the United States has an extremely high rate of incarceration; many criminologists attribute this to the fact that Americans tend to favor harsh punishment for convicted offenders.

SOCIAL NORMS AND SOCIAL CHANGE

In 1993, sociologist and politician Daniel Patrick Moynihan wrote an essay entitled "Defining Deviancy Down," in which he argued that American society was witnessing an extremely high level of deviance and crime, much more than it could "afford to recognize." As a result, he felt, Americans were collectively lowering their standards, and in the process, were coming to accept behaviors that were previously not tolerated. The subtitle of the essay was "How We've Become Accustomed to Alarming Levels of Crime and Destructive Behavior."

If Moynihan's views are right, then a society faced with high levels of deviance will "get used to it" and move to redefine the boundaries of social propriety downward, until an "acceptable" level of deviance is achieved. Indeed, many behaviors considered scandalous (or deviant) in previous decades or centuries are now commonplace: divorce, sexual relations outside of marriage (including same-sex relations), single motherhood, and tattooing. In such cases, the social response to deviance has been to redefine its standards to allow greater latitude in behavior.

On the other hand, sociologists have also studied efforts to redefine social norms in the opposite direction, so that something once permitted or at least condoned would come to be regulated or prohibited. Those most active and vocal in such endeavors are what sociologist Howard Becker called **moral entrepreneurs**—individuals who engage in efforts to persuade the public at large and policy makers that a new rule is needed for the good of society. Their modus operandi is to initiate **moral crusades** aimed at getting society to adopt new norms for social behavior with the underlying purpose of making society "more moral" and less deviant. This endeavor also involves punitive components that range from stigmatization to incarceration. A classic case of moral entrepreneurship is the case of Mothers against Drunk Driving (MADD), a group started in 1980 by a mother whose child was killed by a drunk driver. Prior to the activities of MADD, many U.S. states had relatively lenient drinking and driving laws, and in many states such laws were inconsistently enforced. MADD waged an extensive moral campaign against drunk driving, which resulted in the passage of stricter laws and better enforcement for such laws. As a result, drinking and driving is now stigmatized behavior and the minimum age for drinking has been raised. Moreover, offenders of the new laws face stiffer charges and stiffer penalties. All of these changes can be traced back to the MADD movement.

Public Order Crimes

Public order crimes are offenses that run counter to the established standards of a society, but which do not involve the use of violence or the misuse of property. Such offenses are often called "victimless crimes" or "morality crimes" because there are no clear-cut victims or obvious social harm. These crimes are often related to violations of moral codes of conduct. Examples include vice crimes such as gambling, drug violations, pornography, and prostitution. What characterizes public order crimes is that they seem to spark controversy within society because there is a lack of consensus about the standards relating to these offenses. In addition, many public order crimes involve some perceived benefit for those engaging in the offenses, with the lines between perpetrator and victim blurred or invisible. For example, is the person who buys the crack cocaine as guilty or less guilty than the person who sells it? Who is the guilty party: the prostitute or his/her client? These relationships can even be viewed as business transactions, with one party getting financial compensation and the other party getting a pleasant buzz (or a much-needed fix) or sexual gratification.

Many public order crimes take place in private or surreptitiously, and effective police enforcement of public order laws requires enormous resources, often much more than is available in many jurisdictions. Moreover, few "victims" step forward to alert the criminal justice system that a crime has occurred. In most circumstances, it is hardly likely that the drug purchaser or the prostitute's John will contact police unless something in the "transaction" went very wrong. Consider the implausibility of a drug buyer alerting the police that his or her drug dealer has committed the crime of trafficking in drugs. Such an accusation would include the tacit admission of guilt in purchasing and possessing the same illegal drugs involved in the exchange. Thus, the usual social approach to public order crimes tends to be management—that is, keeping them at reasonably tolerable levels. Managing public order crimes involves a policing style that prevents public order crimes from spreading but does not eliminate them. A second approach to public order crimes (discussed in the following paragraph) is to decriminalize them.

Decriminalization of public order crimes simply means not enforcing laws pertaining to such crimes and is a policy often confused with legalization. The distinction is that decriminalization does not change an existing law but changes how or whether that law is enforced. For example, police may choose not to arrest someone for possession of small amounts of illegal drugs, presumably for individual use. Instead, the police may confiscate the drugs and then release the person without charge. As a practical strategy, decriminalization of certain offenses (e.g., minor drug offenses, prostitution, and gambling) may provide many social benefits. First, decriminalization reduces the strain on the criminal justice system, allowing the system to concentrate on more serious offenses. Second, decriminalization allows citizens to develop their own sense of morality. However, critics of decriminalization argue that failure to enforce existing laws creates an environment of disrespect for law. These critics also argue public order crimes, despite being viewed as victimless crimes, nonetheless cause social harm. Though not always supported with empirical evidence, critics of decriminalization also assert that reducing enforcement will lead to increases in the frequency and intensity of public order crimes.

Laws pertaining to substance use are perhaps the best known examples of public order laws. In the United States, there is a long history of controversy about the use of drugs such as alcohol and narcotics. Over time laws related to both have evolved significantly. American culture values individual control over behavior, and many Americans see drug use as a loss of control, which may lead to undesirable outcomes. In the early part of American history, the consumption of alcoholic beverages (specifically hard cider and beer) was extremely widespread. The low levels of alcohol present in these beverages had potential health benefits, particularly in areas where water sanitation was absent or substandard. However, some religious groups forbade the consumption of alcohol, and various secular temperance movements have worked toward the same goal. Those who opposed alcohol consumption argued that the consumption of spirits lowered the inhibitions of those consuming it and contributed to a variety of social ills. The influence of the temperance movement waxed and waned over time, though the best known period of temperance was the Prohibition Era, when alcohol production and consumption was strictly forbidden in the United States.

Since that time, Americans have become more tolerant of alcohol consumption, and the consensus appears to be that adults should have the individual right to decide whether they will drink or abstain from drinking alcohol. One

Prohibition

In 1919, the U.S. Congress passed the 18th Amendment to the U.S. Constitution, initiating the era of Prohibition. Known as the "Noble Experiment," Prohibition was a legal ban on alcohol production, sale, and consumption. The roots of Prohibition can be traced to earlier religious temperance movements, which sought to ban alcohol by citing various social ills caused by alcohol. Ironically, once alcohol was officially prohibited, an extensive black market emerged, one that allowed organized crime to expand its operations into the production and distribution of illegal alcohol.

During the early years of Prohibition, public opinion was split on the program's effectiveness. But support for Prohibition began to wane as alcohol-related crimes began to escalate. Following the infamous St. Valentine's Day Massacre in 1929, a conflict between two rival gangs during which seven people died, many people who had once felt Prohibition was a good thing began to question the wisdom and the nobility of the "Noble Experiment." In 1933, Congress approved the 21st Amendment, repealing Prohibition.

Drug Scares

The United States is noted for its periodic bout with a phenomenon called *drug scares*, periods of increased social concern about a specific drug or category of drugs, which often result in drug wars and/or anti-drug campaigns. Examples from history include various temperance movements, California's anti-opium movement in the 19th century, an anti-marijuana movement during the Great Depression, and a crack cocaine scare in the 1980s. More recently, we have observed great levels of concern about methamphetamine use in America's rural communities.

Sociologist Craig Reinarman argues that drug scares are a social phenomenon in themselves, a particular aspect of the culture of crime and deviance in the United States, and that all drug scare have common characteristics. Indeed, drug scares are generally based on a kernel of truth, although the ills are almost always exaggerated by the media. Politicians, moral leaders, and professional groups often speak out about the ills of the particular drug that is at the core of the scare, and the drug is linked to a dangerous class of citizens. Finally, the drug becomes the scapegoat for a wide variety of social problems.

Controlled substances such as marijuana are often portrayed as harmful to society. *(Wikipedia)*

of the more recent changes in alcohol laws was prompted by a movement at the end of the 20th century to raise the legal drinking age in the United States from 18 (or 19 in some states) to 21.

Laws pertaining to the use of drugs also reveal how social attitudes toward public order crimes evolve over time. In the early 1900s, many substances that are currently tightly controlled were widely used and marketed. For example, drugs such as opium, morphine, and cocaine could be found in many common products. For example, extracts of the coca leaf were added to Coca Cola, and heroin was sold as a cough suppressant. Over time, critics became more outspoken about the addictions associated with these substances (as well as the resulting social ills), and in the 1920s new laws forbidding the sale of these drugs drove the trade underground.

Since that time, there have been numerous drug scares in the United States, and the criminal justice system has waged a protracted "war on drugs" to reduce the trafficking and sale of illegal drugs. Critics argue that the war on drugs has been ineffective and has led to an unprecedented high rate of incarceration. They contend that the legalization or decriminalization of certain drugs (e.g., marijuana) and a greater emphasis on treatment of addictions (less focus on punishment) would be more effective methods in reducing the social ills caused by drug use.

Social Change and Public Order Crimes

Although everyone agrees that crimes such as murder, rape, and theft should be prohibited, there is a lack of consensus about public order crimes and laws related to these offenses evolve over time. We know that some people in our society agree that illegal gambling, prostitution, and drug use are immoral and may be damaging to society. On the other hand, we also know that a large segment of the population engages in one or all of these behaviors, despite some extensive efforts on the part of law enforcement agencies to curtail these behaviors. In some cases, American culture has become increasingly pragmatic in its view of certain vices. We allow, for example, legal gambling in many states, and state lotteries are not only permitted but encouraged as a way for states to increase revenue from gambling profits. But even beyond the legal forms of gambling, certain types of informal gambling are widely tolerated, such as sports betting pools. As far as gambling is concerned, pragmatism trumps moral outrage, and the United States has responded by legalizing some forms of gambling and ignoring other forms, as long as they are perceived to be innocuous.

On the other end of the spectrum, the United States continues to prohibit prostitution, despite its widespread existence and persistence over time. Prostitution remains illegal in most U.S. jurisdictions, except in some rural counties in Nevada, where prostitution is legalized and regulated. Those who argue prostitution should be legalized (or at least decriminalized) contend that forcing the sex trade underground opens up opportunities for other social problems, including child sex abuse (underage prostitutes), public health problems (when health status of sex workers is not checked or when safe sex practices are not used), human trafficking, and violence against prostitutes. Others rebut these arguments by contending that the normalization of prostitution would not lead to the reduction of related social ills but would instead amplify those ills, leading to even greater exploitation, worsening public health, and greater violence.

A case that falls somewhat in the middle of the "pragmatism vs. morality" continuum is Americans' views of marijuana. Although the sale and possession of marijuana remains illegal in all states, public perception and the criminal justice system have gone through some interesting changes over time. A number of states have decriminalized the possession of marijuana in small quantities, while retaining marijuana laws on the books. Other states have legalized marijuana production, sale, and purchase for medical purposes—by prescription. As a result, national law enforcement agencies and personnel must also decriminalize marijuana use in states with medical marijuana laws. Those who favor decriminalization and/or legalization of marijuana argue that the drug is nearly harmless, and that the enforcement of marijuana laws leads to greater social harm than does the use of marijuana itself. In addition, they cite some therapeutic effects of marijuana and argue that a legitimate marijuana industry can be a source of revenue for government. Critics argue that marijuana is a gateway drug (the idea that marijuana use often leads users to harder, more harmful drugs) and that the marijuana use is linked with physical ailments and psychological problems, such as anxiety and psychosis.

Sociologically, the point of the discussion here is not to argue for or against decriminalization of public order crimes, but to note the variety of social responses that emerge when social behaviors are deemed potentially harmful (or harmless) to the public order. The case of gambling shows that it is possible for a society to become more accepting of a behavior that previously was seen as problematic. On the other extreme is prostitution, which is widespread and persistent, but remains illegal in almost all states. It is interesting to note that American society rejects the idea that prostitution should be legalized and regulated, as it is in many other countries. In the middle is marijuana, which has long been prohibited, but now occupies a moderate position between the two extremes of complete decriminalization (or legalization) and complete prohibition. Together, these three examples help to illustrate the variety of social responses that may be generated following the transgression of social norms.

PARTING WORDS

As we reach the end of this volume, we hope that we have imparted to readers the wide scope of criminal and deviant behaviors and how they are an integral part of the broader social construct. Although many students approach the study of crime and deviance with a great deal of curiosity (often generated by strange cases covered in the entertainment and news media), the study of the rules of social life and their transgression serve as an opportunity to study fundamental aspects of social life. By focusing on the margins between acceptable and unacceptable behaviors, it is possible to learn about social life in general. Indeed, the heart of the matter is the examination of the creation and maintenance of standards for social behaviors, and in the social responses elicited when those standards are violated. Deviance and criminal processes therefore lie at the heart of key sociological concerns: the maintenance of social groups, the performance of rituals to regulate social behaviors, and the broader efforts of a society to define what to allow and what to prohibit. At times, it is possible to focus solely on the negative aspects of crime and deviance, although a broader conception would admit some positive aspects of such behaviors. Although the lion's share of crime may cause real harm and suffering to its victims and the society at large, there are other cases where deviance can be innocuous. In some of its more ideal forms, rule transgression can act as a strong catalyst for social change.

As each of us travels through the social world, it is important to maintain a connection to and a detachment from social life. Certainly, true detachment from one's social perceptions about the rightness (or wrongness) of social behaviors cannot be achieved, and without such an attachment social life might become untenable. On the other hand, many individuals can achieve a level of academic detachment, and such an objectivity concerning the object of study (in this case crime and deviance) can be extremely helpful in understanding the underlying dynamics of behaviors that on the surface may seem confusing or objectionable.

Through this text, I have invited you to act as junior colleagues in the examination of deviance in social life. As we part ways, each of us remains a constant student of social life, a condition necessitated by the fact that we live with the social world. In the final analysis, each of us is responsible for our own behaviors and how we respond to others. When confronted with deviance or criminality (whether our own or someone else's), our disposition toward those behaviors is always our own. It is hoped, however, that this text has armed students with some of the tools needed to view rule transgression within the sociological context.

Further Reading

Becker, Howard S. *Outsiders: Studies in the Sociology of Deviance*. New York: The Free Press, 1963.

Cohen, Stanley. *Folk Devils and Moral Panics: The Creation of Mods and Rockers*. London: MacGibbon and Kee, 1972.

Goode, Erich, and Nachman Ben-Yehuda. *Moral Panics: The Social Construction of Deviance*. Oxford, UK: Blackwell, 1994.

Moynihan, Daniel Patrick. "Defining Deviancy Down." *The American Spectator* 62 (1993): 17–30.

Reinarman, Craig. "The Social Construction of Drug Scares." In *Constructions of Deviance*, 6th ed., edited by Patricia A. Adler and Peter Adler, 155–165. Belmont, Calif.: Thomson Wadsworth, 2009.

Wilson, James Q., and George L. Kelling. "Broken Windows." *The Atlantic Monthly*. March 1982.

GLOSSARY

acquaintance rape   A subcategory of rape involving a perpetrator who is known to the victim.

actus reus   Latin for *guilty act*. A legal term referring to the necessity of an action in the definition of a crime.

aggravated assault   Defined by the FBI as "an unlawful attack by one person upon another for the purpose of inflicting severe or aggravated bodily harm." Assault involves attempting to harm another person or intentionally putting someone in a state of fear by word or deed.

altruism   The selfless concern for the well-being of others, an attitude which has long been the stated standard in many religious traditions.

anorexia nervosa   An eating disorder. Persons affected with this disorder eat an insufficient amount of food and are highly averse to gaining weight.

arson   The intentional unlawful burning of a building (such as a home or place of business), a vehicle, or wild lands.

at-risk youth   Youth whose behaviors or environments make them more likely to become delinquent.

authority conflict pathway   A pathway to delinquency suggested by Rolf Loeber, which begins at an early age (typically prior to age 12) when a child acts in stubborn and defiant ways toward authority figures.

body modification   The intentional alteration of the physical body for nonmedical purposes, including religious expression, self-adornment/aesthetics, as a rite of passage, as an indication of group membership, or for shock value.

bulimia nervosa   An eating disorder. Persons affected by this disorder binge on food and then engage in purging via vomiting and/or taking laxatives.

burglary   Defined by the FBI as the unlawful entering of a residence, place of business, or vehicle with the purpose of committing another felony, characteristically theft.

carjacking   When cars are stolen while the owner is driving the vehicle. Though the event does include a motor vehicle theft, it is primarily considered a robbery, because it involves violence or threat of violence against a person.

child abuse   A category of family violence that involves the physical, psychological, or sexual abuse of a child by parents or other family members.

child protective services   An agency that investigates alleged child abuse and neglect.

choice theories   A variety of theories that focus on the role that independent human decision making plays in determining social behaviors. Choice theory has been a facet of both scientific and common sense thinking about social action since the Age of Enlightenment in the late 18th century.

chop shops   Criminal enterprises where stolen vehicles are stripped of their parts, which are then illegally sold.

civil disobedience   The refusal to obey unjust or immoral laws, rules, or government mandates, typically (though not always) through nonviolent demonstrations or resistance.

civil laws   A subtype of laws that regulate relationships between individuals and are designed to protect the private interests of citizens or groups.

corrections   The branch of the criminal justice system that administers punishments in various forms, including imprisonment, probation, and rehabilitation.

counterculture   A subculture whose norms conflict directly with the norms of the mainstream society. Countercultural groups espouse and live by values that directly contradict the commonly held values in a society.

court   An institution associated with the administration of justice according to the rule of law and according to legally sanctioned procedures. In a practical sense, courts ensure legal fairness and integrity in the processes that determining the legal culpability of offenders and the punishments they should receive.

covert pathway   A pathway to delinquency suggested by Rolf Loeber, which typically begins at age 12 or after and involves the use of concealed deviant behavior (such as lying or shoplifting) that may develop into behavior that damages property (vandalism or arson).

crime   Behavior that is in violation of a criminal law.

crime control   The traditional role of police, which includes preventing criminal acts and apprehending those who break the law.

criminal justice system   A formal network of social institutions charged with enforcement, adjudication, and punishment related to transgressions of law. The criminal justice system includes law enforcement, courts, and corrections; three sets of institutions that work together in responding to crime.

criminal law   A subtype of laws that regulate the behavior of all citizens and is designed to protect the interests of the entire society.

criminogenic   An adjective that describes something that tends to produce crime or criminality. For example, a criminogenic factor would be a factor that tends to produce crime.

criminology   The study of social behavior that violates criminal laws, including its measurement, types, and causes.

cross-dressing   When a person dresses in clothing that does not typically correlate with his or her physiological sex.

dark figure of crime   The amount of crime occurring that is not known to criminologists, specifically crimes not captured even by the best data measuring crime phenomena.

date rape   A subcategory of rape that involves a perpetrator and victim who are in a courtship relationship.

decriminalization   The nonenforcement of laws pertaining to public order crimes. Often confused with legalization, decriminalization does not involve the legalization of public order crimes, but merely involves the reduction or cessation of enforcement for existing laws.

deterrence   The concept that individuals may be discouraged from engaging in norm violating behavior when the penalties for those violations are increased.

deviance   Behavior or attitudes that are in violation of social norms.

deviant beliefs   Values or attitudes that are not accepted by mainstream society. Though they may be accepted in some subcultural circles, deviant beliefs are generally considered odd, undesirable, or repugnant.

deviant identity   Part of the secondary deviance stage, when persons may adopt the attitudes and practices associated with the stigmatized role attributed to them.

differential association   The concept that those who interact more with deviant persons are more likely to adopt their attitudes and behaviors.

discreditable   Deviant acts/statuses capable of being outwardly concealed or disavowed.

discredited Deviant acts/statuses which are either not concealable or have been discovered by, or revealed to, others.

domestic violence Abusive behaviors, whether physical, sexual, or verbal/psychological, within an intimate relationship such as a marriage, domestic partnership, or a dating relationship; also known as domestic abuse, intimate partner violence, and spousal abuse.

eating disorders Unconventional food consumption practices, which include anorexia nervosa and bulimia nervosa. Individuals with eating disorders consume too little or too much food and engaging in other practices related to maintaining certain body weights.

elder abuse A category of family violence in which a person whom an older adult trusts uses that trust inappropriately to abuse the victim. The abuse can include neglect, physical abuse, emotional abuse, sexual abuse, financial abuse, and abandonment.

elder protective services Most counties in the United States have an office of adult protective services, which investigates cases of alleged elder abuse and neglect.

expressive acts Those behaviors intended to communicate some sort of message, whether overt or implied.

external social control Something outside or beyond the individual, which regulates behavior. An example is social sanctioning.

fixing broken windows A community-oriented approach to policing in which police agencies work with communities to clean up signs of deterioration and thereby help residents of crime-ridden communities send a message that crime will not be tolerated.

folkways A type of norms that describe the rules of polite behavior, etiquette, or customary interactions.

forcible rape Commonly defined as an act where a man performs nonconsensual sexual intercourse against a woman. There are other forms of sexual assault, such as male on male, female on female, or female on male, although these acts are not within the traditional concept of rape.

formal social control Responses to deviance undertaken by government agents and formal organizations. These are described in laws or by-laws.

fringe subculture Subcultures that avoid interactions with those in mainstream society.

gender A social category that refers to the roles, attributes, expectations, and behaviors of men and women. Traditional gender roles include the masculine gender role of men and the feminine gender role for women.

grand larceny   Theft involving goods of greater than $50 or $100 in value; often punishable by prison sentences.

groupthink   A phenomenon describing individual members of a group following along with the general sentiment of the group, usually without considering their own preferences. Groupthink is seen more strongly in adolescents than in adults.

harm-based approach   School of thought for studying deviance, which argues there needs to be both an objectively verifiable behavior that causes some actual harm to a person or society in general, and at the same time there must be some subjective awareness of this harm on the part of the members of society.

heteronormativity   The tendency for mainstream society to condone heterosexual preferences and relationships as the norm.

heterosexuality   When men are attracted to women, and vice versa. This is often referred to as "straight sexual orientation."

homicide   See Murder.

homosexuality   When persons are attracted to members of the same sex. Specifically, gay men are attracted to other men, whereas lesbian women are attracted to other women.

informal social control   Responses received from others; the norms violated and the control responses to them may be personal, implicit, or unceremonious in nature.

innovators   A variety of deviants who accept the goals of the wider culture while rejecting the legitimate means for achieving those goals. Innovators develop their own methods for achieving their goals, and often those new ways are rejected by the society.

instrumental acts   Those acts designed to achieve some sort of goal, whether overt or implied.

internal social control   Mechanisms (like conscience and self-control) that regulate behavior from within.

intersex   A medical term that refers to the small proportions of people born with chromosomes, genitalia, or secondary sex traits associated both with males and females.

involuntary manslaughter   Acting with a disregard for harm that might befall another, as in the case of a drunken motorist who kills another person in a vehicle accident. Also known as negligent manslaughter.

juvenile delinquency   Violations of criminal law and other forms of antisocial behaviors committed by youthful offenders, typically those 17 years or younger.

juvenile justice system   First emerged in the mid-19th century; the juvenile justice system aimed to protect youthful offenders from adult offenders and the criminal courts, and to reform youth as productive members of society. The juvenile justice system now includes juvenile courts and juvenile detention centers.

labeling theory   Described by Becker, the idea that deviance is defined by the social identification of behaviors, persons, and attitudes deemed socially undesirable, and through the application of negative labels.

larceny/theft   Defined by the FBI as the unlawful removal of property from the possession of another person.

laws   Norms encompassing the formally written and codified rules of a social group.

LGBTQ   An acronym that means "Lesbian, Gay, Bisexual, Transgender, and Queer/Questioning" and the name of a coalition comprising individuals whose sexual preference, sexuality, or gender identity does not conform to traditional values. LGBTQ groups advocate for the social and civil liberties of those who fit LGBTQ definitions.

mala in se   Latin term meaning *wrong in itself.* Refers to actions that are considered illegal because they are inherently wrong.

mala prohibitium   Latin term meaning *wrong as prohibited.* Refers to behaviors considered illegal because they are determined within the social group to be wrong.

master status   In the secondary deviance stage, an individual may take on the primary identifying social characteristic of a deviant role, whether ascribed or achieved. The master status tends to eclipse all other social characteristics of a person; others interact with that person predominantly via that characteristic.

mens rea   Latin for *guilty mind.* A legal term referring to criminal intent.

moral crusades   The behaviors of moral entrepreneurs as they engage in efforts to persuade the public at large and policy makers that a new rule is needed. Much of moral crusading involves calls to reform or revise formal policies regulating social behavior.

moral entrepreneurs   Those who engage in efforts to get society to adopt a new norm for social behavior. In their behaviors, termed moral crusades, moral entrepreneurs engage in efforts to persuade the public at large and policy makers that a new rule is needed.

moral panic   One of the most extreme forms of control response, characterized by an intensity of emotion and concern expressed by a social group that perceives a threat to its basic social order.

mores Norms that refer to moral rules for behavior.

motor vehicle theft Defined as the unlawful stealing or attempt to steal any motor vehicle, including an auto, truck, motorcycle, or any other motorized vehicle. This property crime is also sometimes known as grand theft auto.

murder Also known as homicide, the unlawful killing of another person with malice aforethought. This means that to be responsible for murder, an offender must have thought about the consequences of the act, no matter how briefly, before committing the act.

National Crime Victimization Survey (NCVS) A telephone survey administered twice per year, which asks respondents to describe the characteristics of any criminal events in which they were victims, including the type of the event, the description of the offenders and victims, the value of property damaged/stolen (if any), and the details of those arrested in connection to the crime.

National Incident-Based Reporting System (NIBRS) A supplement to the UCR (see below); NIBRS allows police to report a greater level of detail about criminal events, including a detailed characteristics of the event, the offenders, victims (if any), value of property damaged/stolen (if any), and the description of the persons arrested for the crime.

negligent manslaughter See Involuntary manslaughter.

non-negligent manslaughter The unlawful killing of another person in the heat of the moment or in a sudden argument, in which the offender's intent to harm the victim is not premeditated. Also called voluntary manslaughter.

normal body image Social norm for what is considered an appropriate or desirable body size, shape, or appearance. Body image may determine whether a person's body is viewed favorably or unfavorably in relation to those standards.

norms The rules of social behavior, which define appropriate behavior in social interactions.

objectivist Employing the assumption that behaviors are either normative or deviant in themselves. This perspective assumes that actions have an independent essence that exists separate from the person(s) committing the act, affected by the act, or interpreting or judging the act.

overt pathway A pathway to delinquency suggested by Rolf Loeber, which typically begins at age 12 or later and involves belligerent acts (e.g., being a nuisance and bullying) that can lead to more serious forms of violence (such as gang involvement, fighting, and robbery).

paranormal beliefs A belief in unlikely and scientifically unverifiable phenomenon (or phenomena).

parens patriae   Latin term meaning *parent of the nation*. A legal term describing state responsibility for children who lack proper parents to raise them, whether because the parents are absent or because the parents, though present, are a negative influence on the child.

Part I property crime   Tracked by the FBI as the four primary forms of property crime: larceny-theft, burglary, motor vehicle theft, and arson. Formerly known as the "property crime index."

Part I violent crime   Tracked by the FBI as the four primary forms of violent crime: murder, rape, aggravated assault, and robbery. Formerly known as the "violent crime index."

petty larceny   Involves theft of objects valued less than $50 or $100 and is punishable by fines or brief jail time. Also known as petit larceny.

police   Agents of the government who are charged with the legitimate duty to enforce laws, protect property, and maintain public order. Typically, police are afforded a monopoly on the legitimate use of force within their geographic boundaries, and police agencies utilize a hierarchical structure that resembles a military chain of command.

prescriptive norms   Those rules of social behavior that describe the actions that are appropriate (i.e., actions that should be taken) in social interactions.

primary deviance   A stage in a deviant career where deviance is not recognized by others and which has little or no effect on the self-identity and social standing of the person practicing the deviance.

problem behavior syndrome   Also known as PBS, a behavioral disposition that refers to a combination of antisocial behaviors or qualities of a youth, which may make the youth more likely to engage in delinquency.

property crime   A crime against material objects, which involves the destruction, misuse, or theft of items of value.

proscriptive norms   Those rules of social behavior that describe actions that are inappropriate (i.e., actions that should be avoided).

public order crimes   Offenses that run counter to the established standards of a society but which do not involve the use of violence or the misuse of property. Such offenses are often known as "victimless crimes" or "morality crimes," because they lack clear-cut victims and social harm; they are often related to violations of moral codes of conduct.

rebels   A variety of deviants who reject both the conventional goals of society and the means for achieving those goals. In rejecting conventional goals and avenues for success, rebels create their own goals and their own methods of achieving those goals.

religious cult   A spiritual group whose practices and beliefs are considered strange by conventional standards. The term "cult" is often perceived as an uncomplimentary label for a religious group.

robbery   Defined by the FBI as "the taking or attempting to take anything of value from the care, custody, or control of a person or persons by force of threat of force or violence and/or by putting the victim in fear." Robbery is a violent offense, not a property crime, because it involves force or intimidation.

routine activities theory   The idea that crime (and hence victimization) occurs most commonly where three factors converge: the presence of motivated offenders, the presence of suitable targets, and the absence of adequate guardians.

secondary deviance   A stage in a deviant career in which deviant behaviors or statuses are recognized and subjected to social control responses. Typically, the deviance is labeled and the person committing the act may also be personally labeled.

secondary victimization   Refers to mistreatment of crime victims that follows the initial victimization, often in the form of shaming, blaming, mistreatment by medical personnel, and poor treatment by criminal justice personnel.

self-injury   Any intentional self-inflicted harm that a person performs on his or her own body.

sex   The physical characteristics of the person, particularly those identifiable characteristics that determine whether the person is male or female.

sexual identity   How a person describes and manifests his or her sexuality, including how that person relates to others. The concept of sexual identity touches upon issues related both to sexual preference and gender performance.

sexual orientation   A term that refers to a person's tendency to develop romantic feelings and sexual attraction toward a specific sex/gender.

social conflict approach   A perspective on deviance that sees the standards for behavior as primarily defined by powerful groups to protect their own interests. Powerful groups often occupy a privileged position in society, one that allows them to exert disproportionately more influence over processes of defining and enforcing standards for social behaviors.

social constructionism   A variety of subjectivist theory, which views the normative sense of society as emerging out of social efforts to define and interpret behaviors. Social constructionists argue that things are appropriate if the social group deems them to be acceptable, just as they are prohibited if the social group agrees that they are unacceptable.

social control   Actions designed to enforce social norms and to regulate behavior.

social stigma   Negative social labels which damage the normalcy of a person's identity in social interactions. Those who have been labeled deviant carry a social stigma.

socialization   A process through which individuals learn the behaviors and attitudes needed for social life within their groups.

status offenses   Behaviors that are prohibited for minors, but which adults can lawfully undertake.

statutory rape   A subcategory of rape that involves an adult having sex with someone below the legal age of consent. Although the legal age of consent varies by state, typically those who are below 14 or 16 years of age cannot legally consent to sexual relations.

structural functionalism   A variety of the objectivist approach, this approach views society as analogous to a biological system in which interdependent institutions fulfill complementary roles that ultimately comprise a coherent system.

structural theories   Theories that focus on factors beyond the control of the individual which determine social behaviors. Structures are typically understood as large scale aspects of social environments and include race/ethnicity, gender, and socioeconomic class.

style cues   Symbolic images in fashion, pop culture, and argot, often employed by subcultures to communicate membership both to insiders and outsiders.

subculture   A social group (overt or covert) whose norms and values differ from those held by the broader culture in which they live. Members of subcultures live by their own norms and values, and therefore the members' sense of what is appropriate may differ greatly from what the society at large considers appropriate.

subjectivist   Employing the assumption that behaviors are not inherently deviant, but are defined as deviant because of the context in which they occur or how they are interpreted. The subjectivist approach assumes that actions have little or no objective essence, and that the rightness or wrongness of the act lies in the details concerning the person(s) committing the act, the person(s) affected by the act, and the person(s) who interpret or judge the act.

suicide   The intentional act of self-injury or potential self-injury where the person undertaking the action cannot be sure of survival. Actual self-killing and attempted/intended self-killing fall both fall under the definition of suicide.

techniques of neutralization   Rationalizations which justify deviant behavior and which are used to help deviant persons maintain a positive outlook toward their self-identity, despite norm violations.

tertiary deviance   A stage in the deviant career where groups embrace their stigmatized labels and then use them as political tools. For example, some groups have learned to value their negative image(s) and have used these stigmas to advocate their own interests.

transgender   Persons who choose to change their social behaviors to conform to the opposite gender's social expectations.

transsexual   Persons who are pursuing, or who have pursued, sex change procedures.

Uniform Crime Reports (UCRs)   Crime reports maintained by the Federal Bureau of Investigation, these include the basic details of every criminal event reported to the police, for example, information about the type of offense and information about both the offender and victim (if any).

victimology   The study of crime victims. Includes one or more of the following areas: understanding the role that the victim plays in the criminal act, understanding types and trends regarding victimization, and understanding the importance of the victim in processes of law enforcement and justice.

victim precipitation   The idea that some crime victims might actually bring about their own victimization by antagonizing the offender. While stopping short of actually blaming persons for their own victimization, this idea is used to indicate the fact that some victims may play a role in encouraging an offender to be abusive (or more abusive).

violent crime   A crime against persons, which involves force, intimidation, coercion, or deception.

voluntary manslaughter   *See* Non-negligent manslaughter.

white supremacy   An extreme form of racial bias or ethnocentrism, centered on the belief that the white race is superior to all other races.

BIBLIOGRAPHY

Becker, Howard. *Outsiders: Studies in the Sociology of Deviance.* New York: The Free Press, 1963.

Brake, Michael. *Comparative Youth Culture.* Boston: Routledge, Keegan & Paul, 1985.

Brown, J. David. "The Professional Ex-: An Alternative for Exiting the Deviant Career." *The Sociological Quarterly* 32 (1991): 219-230.

Chambliss, William J. "The Saints and the Roughnecks." *Society* 11 (1973): 24–31.

Chesney-Lind, Meda. *Girls, Delinquency, and Juvenile Justice.* New York: Wadsworth, 2003.

Cohen, Stanley. *Folk Devils and Moral Panics: The Creation of Mods and Rockers.* London: MacGibbon and Kee, 1972.

Conklin, John. *Why Crime Rates Fell.* New York: Allyn and Bacon, 2003.

Durkheim, Émile. *Suicide: A Study in Sociology.* New York: Free Press, 1997 [1897].

Erikson, Kai. *Wayward Puritans: A Study in the Sociology of Deviance.* New York: Allyn & Bacon, 2004.

Gaines, Donna. *Teenage Wasteland: Suburbia's Dead End Kids.* Chicago: University of Chicago Press, 1998.

Goffman, Erving. *Asylums: Essays on the Social Situation of Mental Patients and Other Inmates.* New York: Anchor Books, 1961.

Goode, Erich. *Paranormal Beliefs: A Sociological Introduction.* Prospect Heights, Ill.: Waveland Press, 2000.

Goode, Erich and Nachman Ben-Yehuda. *Moral Panics: The Social Construction of Deviance.* Oxford, UK: Blackwell, 1994.

Haenflaer, Ross. *Goths, Gamers, & Grrrls.* New York: Oxford University Press, 2010.

Hebdige, Dick. *Subculture: The Meaning of Style.* London: Methuen, 1979.

Marx, Gary T. Ironies of Social Control: Authorities as Contributors to Deviance through Escalation, Nonenforcement and Covert Facilitation. 1974. Chapter available electronically at http://web.mit.edu/gtmarx/www/ironies.html.

Matza, David. *Delinquency and Drift.* New York: John Wiley and Sons, Inc., 1964.

Merton, Robert K. *Social Theory and Social Structure.* New York: Free Press, 1968.

Moynihan, Daniel Patrick. "Defining Deviancy Down." *The American Spectator* 62 (1993): 17–30.

Reinarman, Craig. "The Social Construction of Drug Scares." In *Constructions of Deviance*, 6th ed., edited by Patricia A. Adler and Peter Adler, 155–165. Belmont, Calif.: Thomson Wadsworth, 2009.

Sumner, William Graham. *Folkways: A Study of the Sociological Importance of Usages, Manners, Customs, Mores, and Morals.* Boston: Ginn and Co., 1906.

Sutherland, Edwin. *Principles of Criminology.* Chicago: University of Chicago Press, 1924.

Von Hentig, Hans. *The Criminal and His Victim: Studies in the Sociobiology of Crime.* New Haven: Yale University Press, 1948.

Wilson, James Q., and George L. Kelling. "Broken Windows." *The Atlantic Monthly*, March, 1982.

Wooden, Wayne, and Randy Blazak. *Renegade Kids, Suburban Outlaws: From Youth Culture to Delinquency.* Belmont, Calif.: Wadsworth, 2001.

Zimring, Franklin. *The Great American Crime Decline.* New York: Oxford University Press, 2006.

INDEX

Index note: Page numbers followed by *g* indicate glossary entries.